WHY GLOBALIZATION WORKS FOR AMERICA

WHY GLOBALIZATION WORKS FOR AMERICA

HOW NATIONALIST TRADE POLICIES ARE DESTROYING OUR COUNTRY

EDWARD GOLDBERG

Potomac Books

AN IMPRINT OF THE UNIVERSITY OF NEBRASKA PRESS

© 2020 by Edward Goldberg

All rights reserved. Potomac Books is an imprint of the University of
Nebraska Press.
Manufactured in the United States of America.

∞

Library of Congress Cataloging-in-Publication Data
{~?~CIP to come}
If CIP data does not come in and you must apply for a PCN, this is the
way it should appear in the printed book (omit "Library of Congress
Cataloging-in-Publication Data"):
Library of Congress Control Number: 0000000000

Set in Minion Pro by Laura Ebbeka.

To My Family

But closing the door to the world will not
stop the evolution of the world.

—EMMANUEL MACRON

CONTENTS

Contents

ACKNOWLEDGMENTS

Ironically I owe a debt of gratitude to Donald Trump and Bernie Sanders. During the 2016 campaign for the presidency of the United States, their never-ending simplistic attacks on globalization as well as Trump's actions after he was elected made me realize the need for a straightforward argument demonstrating how globalization benefits the United States. How nationalistic, isolationist-like trade policies especially in the age of globalization are extremely detrimental to our country's economic health.

I also am grateful to my students at New York University's Center for Global Affairs. Every Thursday afternoon they challenge my ideas on globalization and its impact on American foreign policy and in the teaching process help me to clarify my thinking.

In addition I wanted to thank Thomas Quinn, who was a brilliant graduate student of mine at the Center for Global Affairs. Tom did an excellent job in assisting me on the research for the book.

I am very grateful to my agent, Carol Mann, of the Carol Mann Agency, whose encouragement, judgment, handholding, and persistence makes her all an author could wish a literary agent to be. I was also fortunate to have had a wonderful and knowledgeable editor, Tom Swanson, at Potomac Books. It was a pleasure to work with Tom and with his associates Abigail Stryker and Haley Mendlik. Wayne Larsen's copyediting was very perceptive and precise.

I also need to thank Barbara Monteiro and Len Maniace of Monteiro and Company for their handholding and hard work throughout this project.

Last, I am so grateful to my wife, Barbara G. Saidel, for her steadfast support, honesty, wise counsel, and, most important, her love.

WHY GLOBALIZATION WORKS FOR AMERICA

Introduction

> I am sure that the power of vested interests is vastly
> exaggerated compared with the gradual
> encroachment of ideas.
>
> —JOHN MAYNARD KEYNES

In my book *The Joint Ventured Nation: Why America Needs a New Foreign Policy*, I wrote about how America's foreign policy needed to adjust to a globalized world, how the role of the United States in the international arena needs to evolve from that of indispensable nation to that of indispensable partner—and how America can remain first among equals in a joint ventured world.

Why Globalization Works for America is not about foreign policy; it is about the nine-hundred-pound gorilla named globalization that has reshaped the United States. It is about why globalization is here to stay, why America is the winner in the game of globalization, and why all the king's horses and all the king's men can't put the Humpty Dumpty of yesterday's nonglobalized world back together again.

This book is not about Donald Trump. It is about the tsunami of economic and cultural forces that swept Donald Trump into office. Whether Trump remains in office or not, he is merely a manifestation of the change-based economic discontent that will not rapidly dissipate when he leaves.

Globalization is a natural part of the human condition. It is the economic, political, and cultural version of evolution. Globalization is not a new phenomenon; it existed thousands and thousands of years before Tom Friedman wrote *The World Is Flat*. As the Israeli historian Yuval Noah Harari points out in *Sapiens: A Brief History of Humankind*, "Cultures began swallowing and absorbing others from the earliest times of history."

Just look at the history of the tomato in Italy. The tomato, which is emblematic of Italian cuisine, is not Italian at all but Peruvian. Its arrival in Europe during the Renaissance defines globalization. The tomato originated in the Andes Mountains, traveled to Mexico, where it became part of Aztec cuisine, and was brought to Spain by the returning conquistadors in the 1500s. Shortly afterward it appeared in Italy, where it was reportedly first used by Cosimo de' Medici not in a sauce but as an ornamental item. Because it was red, the Italians at that time would not eat it, believing it was the devil's food. For its part, pasta—another defining dish of Italy—appears to have originated in Greece and the Middle East, and was brought to Italy not by Marco Polo as the myth states but by Arab traders.

The United States is a child of globalization, born during one of globalization's earlier incarnations, the European Age of Discovery. Globalization is part of America's DNA. To try to separate globalization from America would be like separating a child from its mother.

Long before the current term *globalization* became popular, the United States as a country defined the word. Founded by a mixture of cultures—whether British in New England, Dutch in New York, French in New Orleans, or Spanish in its West—the United States then opened its doors in the mid to late nineteenth century to massive immigration from all over the world. In the second half of the twentieth century, the United States not only created the rules that allowed the current era of globalization to spread around the world; it also became the enforcer of those rules.

And America was—and still is—the biggest winner in the current era of globalization. Of course, a country like China that was in abject poverty became rich because of globalization, but America became even wealthier. In a globalized world, however, trade is only a zero-sum game in the negative when major economies become poorer and drag their trading partners down with them.

Take a look at what happened since 1980, when globalization first started to be a major factor. The United States at that time had a gross domestic product (GDP) of $2.8 trillion, while China's was only $302 billion. By 2019, however, the World Bank estimated that the U.S. economy grew to $20.4 trillion while the Chinese economy grew to $14.1 trillion. As you can see, the U.S. economy grew massively during that period, even taking into account the crash of 2008. Of course, China's rate of growth during the same time was much higher, but that is just basic common sense. If you start with very little, you need to catch up. China needed to build steel mills and highways, and to electrify their rural areas. The United States did all that a long time ago. The point is that the United States did not get poorer as China grew—quite the opposite.

Since China started at practically zero when globalization began, its winnings look much more impressive to the outside world than reality shows. In the aggregate of course, China has become a much wealthier country, but on a per capita basis it is still very poor compared with the United States. For example, in 2018 China's per capita GDP was, according to the World Bank, only $9,770, compared with $62,461 for the U.S. By this standard, even Greece, Europe's most troubled economy with a per capita income of $20,324, is wealthier than China. But while China was getting richer, American consumers on the whole—and especially the lower-middle class who tend to spend a greater percentage of their incomes on basic goods—benefited enormously from globalization. As an example, look at a basic item like baby and toddler clothes. According to Pietra Rivoli, a trade expert at the McDonough School of Business at Georgetown University, because of imports the price of these items dropped by 10 percent from 1999 to 2013. And according to the Dallas Fed, Americans saw their choice of products expand by one-third in recent decades on account of globalization. Just look at the variety of fruits and vegetables at one's local grocery store, even during the middle of winter.

But cheap baby clothes are only relevant politically if you have something to compare them with, and the aggregate growth of the United Sates GDP is totally irrelevant if you are fifty years old and cannot adapt to changes in the economy. And so something very radical happened: the United States—ignoring its own history—constitutionally elected an antiglobalization president. A counter-revolution against globalization had been growing rapidly around the world, and on November 8, 2016, those forces captured the U.S. presidency.

Employing the rhetoric of anger and disillusionment, Donald Trump and the antiglobalization forces were able to reduce the complex subject of globalization to the simple perception that America's elitist leadership had sold out to the forces of globalization as it marched through the country, destroying jobs, challenging America's right to freely act in the world, and letting immigrants—the other—in. The spin-makers of the counterrevolution had aggressively popularized the idea that world growth is a zero-sum game, and since China's economy had grown substantially over the past forty years, it had to mean that the U.S. economy has declined substantially. And by implication the international norms fostered by America's so-called elites since the fall of the Soviet Union were in fact traitorous to the American people.

We know that there is no record of a counterrevolution against the tomatoes during the Renaissance. But possibly, that is because the tomato went gradually from being a table ornament to a staple of the Italian diet. Gradual globalization is a true natural human phenomenon. The difference now is the speed of change, as we no longer have the option of centuries to adapt or even decades but—at best—months before there is new change. The purpose of this book is twofold: first to show, how—within this climate of speed—the counterrevolution against globalization that feeds on the inability of people to rapidly adapt to change will fail, and second, why globalization is both necessary and bound to succeed.

America's enemy is not globalization; America's enemy is America. The anger that fostered America's counterrevolution against globalization derived from the fact that the benefits of globalization were not shared throughout all regions of the country, that there was a severe breakdown in how the American system responded to revolutionary changes in the economy. During previous periods of massive economic upheaval and change—such as the Industrial Revolution and the Great Depression—American democracy united to reform and reinvigorate the system. There was no similar response this time to support those who were hurt by the massive changes in the economy brought on by globalization. There was never even a full political discussion about how to harness globalization for the benefit of all; laissez-faire simply won without a fight.

Look how differently China and the United States perceive the benefits of globalization. President Xi of China went to the World Economic Forum in Davos, Switzerland, in January of 2017 and easily praised globalization. Of course, he leads a country where just about everyone over the past forty years benefited greatly from globalization. Whether it is the fifty-year-old Chinese peasant who remembers living without running water, or the hundreds of millions of people who have moved into a Chinese version of middle-class life, or the over one million people who now have assets of over a million dollars, China's citizenry as a whole benefited from globalization. In contrast, two months before Xi's speech in Davos, Donald Trump was able to win the presidency on an antiglobalization platform by exploiting the deep range of anger felt by the many Americans who had been left out of America's Manhattanized globalization boom.

The 2016 election brought into daylight two sharp fissures in the American electorate created by globalization. The first was between the "newocracy," America's new aristocracy, the beneficiaries of globalization—including the multinational manager, the technologist, and the aspirational members of the meritocracy—and the "refugees from globalization." This, in fact, is America's real refugee problem: middle-class American industrial workers who no longer have the job skills to maintain their previous lifestyles in a globalized world.

The other major fissure is between industries, between the old industries of steel and coal and the new globalized human-capital-based industries of artificial intelligence and e-commerce. What has made the United States the principal creator of the knowledge age is its ability to adapt to change—an ability derived from the United States' cultural respect for the freedoms to take risks, to innovate, and to be entrepreneurial. Innovation, however, by definition brings about change, creating winners and losers.

In the American economic and political system, the notion that government and industry are totally independent of each other is a simplistic myth. How long the losers survive, and how quickly the winners can grow, is partly determined by which industries get government support and protection, and which do not. For instance, the old-line industries want government protection from imports with penalizing duties, while the new industries want free trade. Where "Made in America" is an important slogan for U.S. Steel, Apple relies similarly on global sourcing and the global exchange of ideas. Consider the industrial leaders who backed President Trump and are in his cabinet; they are primarily investors in the old fixed-asset economy of America, while the new leaders of American corporate life, the Silicon Valley of America, primarily backed Hillary Clinton.

But although the old industries won the election in 2016, they had already lost the war. Globalization, the breeding ground for the new industries, is not going back into the genie's bottle. Consider the Trump protectionist crusade against China in support of American steel at the start of his administration and ask yourself which side will eventually win. The steel industry in the United States in 2016 employed one-tenth of 1 percent of the American workforce, approximately eighty-seven thousand workers, while ironically the steel-importing industry employed over sixty thousand workers in the United States. Without a doubt, the steel industry over the past twenty years has been hemorrhaging workers. These numbers have little to do with imports, however, instead being based on automation. The truth is that in the late 1970s, it took ten workers to make a ton of steel, while today it takes only one.

Compare the steel industry with the American auto industry, a truly globalized player, with its integrated global sourcing, manufacturing, and marketing. China is now General Motors' largest market, with eleven joint-venture plants in China that produced and delivered more than 3.8 million vehicles in 2018, compared to 2.9 million in the United States. Or look at Apple, whose second-largest market is in China. A trade war with China to protect the U.S. steel industry would almost certainly threaten GM and Apple. A trade war might make sense as political rhetoric to feed the base, but in reality it is a nonstarter.

Furthermore, consider Boeing, in many ways the crown jewel of American sophisticated manufacturing. Although it assembles its planes in the United States, it sources the parts for these planes from all over the world. Parts for Boeing's 787 Dreamliner come from five thousand factories worldwide. The forward fuselage comes from Japan, the engines from England, the entry doors from France, and the rudder from China. The Boeing 787 might be trademarked "Made in America," but in the air it is the flying definition of globalization, a true mutt.

The 787 represents another sharp contrast between the old industries and the new. The new industries straddle globalization, seeing the world itself as the marketplace, understanding that in order to sell to the world, they need to buy from the world. Boeing would need to shrink tremendously as a company to be a supplier of just domestic commercial aircraft, as approximately 70 percent of Boeing Commercial Airplanes' revenue comes from customers outside the United States. To sell to the world and not create local foreign pressure to build competing commercial aircraft factories, Boeing recognizes that it must share the wealth by sourcing across the world.

Accentuating the divide between the newocracy and the refugees of globalization—and between the new industries and the old—is the fact that the United States and the world have entered the age of human capital. Since the invention of the spinning jenny in 1764, manufacturing and the people it employs have been the underlying basis of all modern economies and the foundation of America's middle class. This status is no longer so. The world is shifting very rapidly from the manufacturing age to the age of human capital, a shift in many ways similar to the change from the Bronze Age to the Iron Age. The difference is that today's change is happening not over centuries but literally overnight.

As the world moves further away from the age of manufacturing, the loss of manufacturing jobs because of automation and technology has become a rallying cry against globalization, even though the connection is tenuous.

Globalization had nothing to do with all the jobs lost in upstate New York by people who used to make Brownie cameras. Does anyone buy a Brownie camera anymore? Additionally, globalization has nothing to do with the department stores that can no longer compete against Amazon, or with your neighborhood supermarket, where cashiers have been replaced by scanners. If there is one thing that is difficult to build a wall around, it is automation.

But beyond the rapid changes in technology, a basic human factor has affected globalization's appeal: the bloom is off the rose. The original halcyon hopes of the early 1990s have given way to a much more realistic view not only of the positive elements of globalization but also of the potential negatives.

The 1990s were a period of elation, as the Cold War had ended, borders were opening, and global unity was increasing. Technology was not yet a threat but rather an exciting vision of tomorrow: the IBM Thinkpad laptop had just gone on the market, and more than four million Apple 2 computers had been shipped by 1993. And 9/11—the horrific punctuation mark that continues to shape our public lives—had not yet occurred. The 1990s were also a time of increased prosperity, when a rising tide was lifting most boats. Warren Buffett has an expression: "Only when the tide goes out do you discover who's been swimming naked." So it was to be with globalization. Before 9/11, before the financial crisis of 2008, before terrorism in western Europe—all related to the downside of globalization—the underbelly of the globalized kumbaya was not apparent. Now the tensions of fear created by these events—fueled by the speed of technological change—has ignited the counterrevolution against globalization.

This book explores how America and the world it created are now in a war between yesterday and tomorrow. America, along with the concept of globalization, is now at a severely destabilizing crossroads. From the time the current era of globalization began to emerge, it was assumed that because globalization generally made societies wealthier, governments would support policies that enhanced global interaction and growth. This assumption has now hit a political wall of nationalism, fear, and economic discontent. America—essentially the creator of globalization—is now cannibalizing the system it created. Globalization has been overshadowed by xenophobia, while the lessons of history have been abruptly ignored.

Beneath all the noise, however, globalization continues to move forward. Globalization, as described by the State University of New York's Levin Institute, "is a process of interaction and integration among the people, companies, and governments of different nations, a process driven by international trade and investment and aided by information technology." The World Economic Forum adds to this statement by including this statement: "Globalization [is] also a cultural element, where traditions are traded and assimilated." These definitions, however, ignore one of the most basic points about globalization: the negative. Historically, countries that block globalization at their border wither. This truism has affected all nations, whether it was the withdrawal of the great fleet and restrictions on shipbuilding by the Ming Dynasty in China in the middle of the fifteenth century, the emperor's fear of building railroads in the Austro-Hungarian Empire in the nineteenth century, or the insularity of the Soviet Union late in the twentieth century.

The United States, by directly and indirectly promoting globalization, has been the major winner in reaping the benefits of globalization. And there is no reason to believe, even with an antiglobalist administration, that the United States won't continue to be globalization's biggest medal holder. So in chapter 1, titled "Big Victory but No Parade," I look at why globalization is worth it, why it works for the United States, and why the United States economically and culturally has been the beneficiary of globalization since its founding as a nation.

Chapter 1 is about many things: how today Americans love eating clementines from Spain in the middle of winter, or being able to afford a pair of Nikes, or shopping at Ikea, or driving around in a Japanese Toyota Camry made in Georgetown, Kentucky. It is about how essentially real globalization in the United States, not the globalization of political rhetoric, suffers from the curse of ubiquitousness. And most importantly it is about why globalization is so advantageous to the United States as a whole, and why the United States should continue to be the winner in the game of globalization.

Just look at the May 6, 2017, cover of the *Economist* magazine, published a little over three months after Donald Trump was inaugurated. While Trump rambled on about how globalization has hurt America, the magazine had on its cover a headline declaring, "The World's Most Valuable Resource," under which was a drawing of the logos of Google, Amazon, Uber, Microsoft, Facebook, and Tesla sitting on top of what could be offshore oil platforms. The implication is that now, a country's most valued resource is its ability to globally apply its human capital, rather than assets like oil and natural gas. Most notable is that the *Economist*, a global magazine, chose only U.S. companies for this cover.

Both economically and politically, globalization has not only worked for the United States but shown amazing staying power. Instead of surrendering to populism after the horrors of the 2008 crash, America twice elected a non-Caucasian intellectual globalist as its president. Then, in 2016—with the typical pendulum swing of politics reinforced by the Democrats not having the most popular candidate—Donald Trump became president, not by winning the popular vote but by prevailing through a quirky 1787 constitutional provision, ironically formulated to put a check on popular, or what we would today call populist, democracy.

In chapter 2, "Make It Like It Was," I look at the three major reasons why the counterrevolution against globalization is failing and why it will continue to fail.

Politics is the art of perception. Ed Koch, the late mayor of New York, recalled that while he was campaigning on the Coney Island boardwalk in Brooklyn, an elderly woman approached him and implored that he "make it like it used to be." America today is richer than it has ever been and is in the healthiest condition of any major global economy, yet many Americans don't see it that way. Like Ed

Koch's elderly constituent, they want it to be like it used to be. And globalization gets caught up in that.

The counterrevolution against globalization is trapped within its own rhetoric. Politically, it is easy to exploit the anger of people who have been left behind by globalization, but it is impossible to demonstrate how the country and the world would be better off without globalization. It is also easy to confuse—and deliberately conflate—the economic changes brought on by the technological revolution with the changes wrought by globalization. But the counterrevolution against globalization has always historically failed. In the wonderful book *Why Nations Fail: The Origins of Power, Prosperity, and Poverty*, by Daron Acemoglu and James A. Robinson, the authors tell the fascinating story about how both the Austro-Hungarian emperor and the czar of Russia tried to limit railroad construction in the nineteenth century, out of fear that radical "foreign ideas" would spread in their empires. Fearing industrialization and commerce that would threaten the emperor's absolute control, Austrian emperor Francis I—when approached with the idea of building a northern railroad in the country—stated, "No no, I will have nothing to do with it, lest the revolution might come into the country." Of course, we all know how successful that was.

In chapter 3, "A Disturbance in the Force," I look at how the American political system failed, allowing the counterrevolution against globalization to become a potent political force. Why did this happen? Specifically, how did the American political system not see the harm globalization was causing to a significant minority of the U.S. population? Why didn't the system see what could be called—to use a term from *Star Wars*—"a great disturbance in the force?" Why didn't it act to restrain and harness globalization? Why was the political system in the United States so deaf to how America was changing? And why did it take until the election of 2016 to see that a severe political crisis had developed? After all, globalization as we know it is not a recent phenomenon; it began to affect American workers in the 1980s.

During the industrial revolution in the late nineteenth and early twentieth centuries, the administrations of Theodore Roosevelt, William Howard Taft, and Woodrow Wilson initiated reforms to stop the American industrial revolution from morphing into a monopolized aberration of capitalism. And thirty years later, Franklin Roosevelt—confronted by the Great Depression—created a safety net for American workers to partially protect them from the inevitable downsides of capitalism. During both periods, the American government expanded its powers to adjust to situations that could never have been foreseen when the Constitution was ratified in 1788. So if there was a pattern for the U.S. government to intervene during periods of massive economic change, why didn't that happen with globalization?

Chapter 4, "How *Downton Abbey* Resonates in America Today," is about how the 2016 election was much more than just a fight about how disgruntled workers in Michigan, Indiana, or Pennsylvania were supposedly hurt by globalization. It was also a major battle for government support between the old industries, whose roots go back to America's first industrial revolution, and America's new globalized human capital industries.

Just look at the representatives of industry in Trump's cabinet vis-à-vis the people who backed Hillary. But—like the counterrevolution itself—even though the candidate of the old industries won the election, the reality is the old industries have already lost the war. Trump's supporters have been given some short-term government goodies, whether through higher tariffs or tax support, but in the long term will this be enough for these companies to continue to flourish and survive. Ask yourself which is more important to the U.S. economy today: Apple, which has little influence on any specific electoral votes, or the coal and steel industry, which influences the electoral votes of Kentucky, West Virginia, and Pennsylvania? Globalization has been fully integrated into the most dominant aspects of the American economy, whether aerospace or agriculture, computers or finance, and all the talk about protectionism and the evils of various trade pacts won't change that fact.

Consider the North American Free Trade Agreement (NAFTA), which Donald Trump railed against throughout the campaign. In Kenosha, Wisconsin, on April 18, 2016, he said, "NAFTA's been very,

very bad for our country. It's been very, very bad for our companies and for our workers, and we're going to make some very big changes, or we are going to get rid of NAFTA once and for all. Cannot continue like this, believe me." But after the election, when it came to governing, globalization won. Reality set in. Whether it was behind-the-scenes congressional pressure from the farm states or someone just telling Trump the obvious facts—such as that Mexico is one of the top three markets for U.S. agriculture or that General Motors is much more competitive because of its integrated Mexican supply chain—NAFTA was not torn up. Instead Trump followed the comma theory of political negotiation. Yell loudly, change some commas and minor details in the very technical NAFTA treaty that the common citizen doesn't understand, and declare victory.

Chapter 5, "Becoming Less Great," is about what happened to America's global leadership. It is about how the leaders of the United States was so caught up in America as the post–Cold War Rome that they failed to see how globalization was changing the ways countries relate to each other. The Cold War had ended, but the mindset of America's leaders saw only old-fashioned realpolitik and not the rapidly changing, all-encompassing globalized economy.

For historical change to become successfully embedded in global political culture, it must be sanctified by the leading power of the time. This rule has been true throughout history, whether it was the Roman emperor Constantine's acceptance of Christianity or the U.S. blessing the economic integration of western Europe via the post–World War II Marshall Plan. The ability of the hegemon, the global leader, to be the role model and accept change becomes the impetus for the success of that change.

Certain elements of post–Cold War American leadership—in particular the neoconservatives prominent in the administration of George W. Bush—didn't see globalization as a positive change to support, or even as something to harness for America's benefit. They denied it outright, governing on a rigidly ideological worldview that beheld the United States as the sole center of world power. The neoconservative worldview had more in common with Hans Christian Andersen's "The Emperor's New Clothes" than with reality. There are myriad examples of their myopia: the cancellation of the antiballistic missile treaty with Russia, the decision not to be a party to the Kyoto treaty on global warming, and the commission set up by the Pentagon to study what it called "pivotal hegemonic powers in history'" to determine how the U.S. could maintain its advantage in the twenty-first century. By the time President Bush left office, their philosophy had a devastating negative influence on the growth of political globalization.

Nationalism begets nationalism, especially when sponsored by the hegemon. Consequently, when the United States determined that its interests could be better served with a more go-it-alone strategy, it implicitly sanctioned the rights of other countries to withdraw from the globalized roundtable. In subtle and not so subtle ways, other countries and populaces began to understand that it could now be beneficial to discourage the centripetal forces of globalization.

The changes globalization made to sovereignty, economies, and individual livelihoods would invariably have produced some global backlash, as traditional cultural fault lines were being threatened, but that backlash could have been somewhat mitigated if the American hegemon had used its influence and power to accept globalization and channel it. Instead, nationalism was reignited globally, along with isolationism within America, effectively creating a new global tower of Babel.

In chapter 6, "We Have Nothing to Fear but Fear Itself," I look at how technology and social media spurred on by, and playing off of, globalization, disrupted the political order far beyond what anyone could have ever imagined. As the *Smithsonian* magazine pointed out, "When faced with transformational technologies, people are afraid of losing things: cultural identities, ways of life, or economic security. In nineteenth-century England, for instance, the Luddites destroyed textile machines in order to preserve their jobs and livelihoods, not out of a stubborn aversion to technology."

This chapter looks at the death of our own Industrial Age. Since the advent of the industrial revolution in England, the dominant factor in the global economy until very recently had been manufacturing. We have now entered the age of human capital, and the adjustment to this new age—with its different skill sets and needs—is traumatic. The change is apparent everywhere. For example, in 2014 international trade added $7.8 trillion to the global economy. For the first time, however, data flows—with a value of $2.8 trillion—represented a higher proportion of that figure than goods, which represented $2.7 trillion.

The decline in the value of manufacturing and, by extension, the decline in the need for workers to manufacture products have caused a fundamental economic and political transformation, sending populist shockwaves around the world. But technology and globalization are not synonymous, and in the United States, where technology and innovation are considered part of America's DNA, it became politically much easier to attack globalization and the other than to blame technology. In fact, blaming globalization for cultural changes in America caused by technology predates Donald Trump by almost ninety-six years. As I show in the chapter, the 1920s was a period very similar to today. Significant technological changes disrupted American society in the 1920s, and political leaders, wanting to pacify their constituents, falsely and damagingly blamed the outside world and instituted nationalist trade policies that led to economic ruin.

I conclude with chapter 7, "Tomorrow." It is about not the victory of globalization, which is inevitable, but instead the damage the counterrevolution will do to America and the world. Before the revolt against globalization fizzles out, as previous counterrevolutions have done, will it—infused by the entropic, countercylindrical forces of social media—lead to isolationism, increased authoritarianism, the end of the American experiment of a multiethnic democracy, and the end of America's cornucopia of wealth?

What happens if and when America knowingly cedes the leadership of globalization to China? Does globalization go from a game that benefited most people around the world to one, absent American leadership, called "One Road to China"?

In a world satiated with technology yet short of natural resources, where globalization has caffeinated the massive societies of China and India and parochialism is in open rebellion, will the counterrevolution lead to a period combining pre–World War I economic nationalism with some new form of authoritarianism? Or can globalization, which has truly been beneficial not only to the majority of Americans but also to the world, be harnessed to preserve democracy as we know it? At the moment, we are in a race between democracy and authoritarianism, between globalization and nationalism. Globalization will win as it has always done, but how democracy finishes in this race is another question entirely.

ONE

Big Victory but No Parade

America is truly the lucky country. With its temperate climate, fertile plains, raw materials, river system, natural harbors, and oceans protecting its east and west borders, it has won the geographic lottery. But it also won the globalization lottery. I have a good friend who often says, "You make your luck." In the nineteenth century America did just that and benefited from globalization like no other country in the world. Now, in the beginning of the twenty-first century, because of its culture, history, and the ability to see opportunities, the United States is again the true winner in a new, much faster version of the game of globalization.

From the Levi's jeans that retail for around $128—which would be $348 if made in the United States—to affordable Nikes, iPhones, and TVs, where a similar price ratio applies, to clementines, pineapples, and tomatoes that magically appear in the supermarkets in the winter, twenty-first-century globalization has stealthily become synonymous with life in the United States. The problem in fact is that globalization, not the political term but the reality, has become such a common part of American lives that it suffers from the curse of ubiquitousness.

Globalization has become so ubiquitous that most Americans are totally nonchalant when it comes to its ever-increasing presence. Just look at professional sports in America. By opening day of the baseball season in 2017, over 29 percent of the players were born outside the United States. Or look at the National Basketball Association, the NBA, where a third of the players are not American. What is amazing is that these facts are no longer even a news story. Compare today with 1947, when Jackie Robinson, an American, not someone who was foreign born, was spit on and cursed at simply because as a black person he was playing in the major leagues.

Or look at the automobile industry and the cars we drive. If one drives a Volkswagen, made by a German company, there is a good chance the car was manufactured in either Mexico or the United States. Likewise, buying a Honda, a Japanese brand, does not necessarily mean buying a Japanese car, as it is very possible the car was assembled in one of Honda's twelve factories in the United States. The same goes for the German BMW. Even General Motors—the king of the American car industry—now has thirteen plants in China and a distribution network of fifty-one hundred dealers there. Meanwhile, Mercedes, the crown jewel of German manufacturing, is building SUVs in Indiana for sale in China.

Beyond clementines and tomatoes, globalization has become even more pervasive in American culture. According to Yelp, there are more than sixteen sushi restaurants in Fairbanks, Alaska, and twenty in Wichita, Kansas. Wichita also has seven Indian restaurants. Grand Rapids, Michigan, has eighteen Japanese restaurants, and Biloxi, Mississippi, has seventeen. And Red Bull—an Austrian energy drink—has sales in the United States approaching $1 billion.

The ubiquitousness of globalization has made it an easy political enemy to attack. Practically all Americans enjoy the benefits of globalization, but few realize that globalization has been the instigator of these benefits. Most people are not even aware that the Honda they drive or the clementines they eat or the comparatively inexpensive clothing they wear would come under the definition of globalization.

It is deceptively easy for Americans to believe that world trade and growth are a zero-sum game, and that for China to get rich, America had to get poorer. But that is just not so, although it is both counterintuitive and impossible to explain in a political sound bite. In 1980, approximately when our current period of globalization started to take off, the United States had a gross domestic product of $2.8 trillion, while China's was only $302 billion. By 2019 the

U.S. economy's GDP was estimated to be $20.4 trillion, while the Chinese economy had an estimated GDP in dollars of $14.1 trillion.

The U.S. economy grew massively during that period, even taking into account the crash of 2008. Of course, China's rate of growth during the same period was much higher, but that is just common sense. If you start with very little, you need to catch up. China needed to build steel mills and highways, and to electrify their rural areas. The United States did all that a long time ago. The point is that the United States did not get poorer as China grew—quite the opposite, it got substantially wealthier.

In this context, "substantially wealthier" is definitely a macroeconomics term, meaning that it deals with the economy as a whole. Certainly, many Americans did not see any increase in their wealth, and some have seen a decrease. Globalization is in this case purely an economic force; how the winnings and losses are distributed and how the people who have been hurt by globalization are compensated are political issues, which I will discuss in chapter 3.

Globalization is not new. It is part of the human condition. In some form or another, it can be seen in Joseph's going into Egypt, Alexander of Macedonia's influence on global culture, and as I wrote in the introduction, the tomato's arrival in Italy via Mexico and Spain. And globalization is definitely not new to the United States. Only the word is new. The United States is a child of globalization. It was born during one of globalization's earlier incarnations, the European age of discovery. Globalization is part of America's DNA. To try to separate globalization from America would be like separating a child from its mother.

And here we get back to the tomato story, where the introduction of the tomato into the United States not only is an example of that earlier period of globalization but also shows how from the beginning of the country, globalization and its changes blended into the character of the nation. Our well-traveled tomato did not come to the United States via Mexico, where it was part of the Aztec diet and which would logically be the direct source. Instead, John de Sequeyra, a British-Portuguese doctor, brought it to Williamsburg, Virginia, from Europe in the 1740s. By 1781 the tomato had become a common vegetable in Virginia. Thomas Jefferson wrote in his *Notes on the State of Virginia*, "The gardens yield musk melons, watermelons, tomatoes, okra, pomegranates, figs, and the esculent plants of Europe." As you can see Jefferson does not single out the tomato as being a newly imported plant or something out of the ordinary. In other writings, however, he does credit Dr. Sequeyra for being the first to bring the tomato to Virginia. By the way, besides introducing the tomato to the American colonies, Dr. Sequeyra became one of the first physicians in what would later become the United States to seriously treat the mentally ill.

From its beginning the United States—whose early motto was "E pluribus unum" (out of many, one)—defined the word *globalization*. Founded by a mixture of cultures—whether British in New England, Dutch in New York, French in New Orleans, or Spanish in its West—the United States then opened its doors in the middle to late nineteenth century to massive immigration from all over the world. As Jason Zweig of the *Wall Street Journal* pointed out, "America [was] named for an Italian, farmed by Scots & Scandinavians, built by Irish & Chinese & Poles [and I would add Africans]."

But it was not just the mixture of cultures that made the United States historically synonymous with what we now call globalization. Most definitions of globalization begin with the phrase "a process driven by international trade and investment." International investment has been key to the growth of the United States since its founding. Probably no other country, except possibly modern-day Israel, has benefited as much from international investment throughout its history as the United States.

It is not too much of a stretch to say it would have been difficult for the United States to exist as a country without these investments. During the American War of Independence, Benjamin Franklin negotiated a loan from France to the Continental Congress for $2 million, while John Adams secured a loan with various bankers in Amsterdam for five million guilders. In addition, the French government covertly began to ship war materials to the Continental Congress as early as 1775 through a series of dummy corporations that received French funds and used them to buy military supplies.

The American government began with the same international interlocking government debt that is now normal in our current age of globalization. In 1789, the year of the first presidential election in the United States, the foreign debt of the new government was 29 percent of the government's obligations. And this figure does not take into account debt held by individual states and American corporations, which was also sizable. As a comparison, according to the Congressional Research Service, in 2018, 39 percent of the U.S. government debt was held by overseas entities.

It was the purchase of the Louisiana territory, however, from France in 1803 that firmly cemented the United States' status as a child of globalization. The Louisiana Purchase doubled the land size of the United States, and could not—and would not—have taken place without the use of foreign capital markets. At a cost of $15 million the purchase was the largest financial transaction of the time. The land President Jefferson acquired from France was vast: 828,000 square miles that included what is now the states of Arkansas, Missouri, Iowa, Oklahoma, Kansas, and Nebraska, as well as parts of North Dakota, South Dakota, New Mexico, Texas, Montana, Wyoming, Colorado, and Louisiana, including the city of New Orleans.

The bonds to fund the purchase of the territories were issued mainly by two banks, Barings of London and Hope and Company of Amsterdam. It was the first significant time that U.S. securities were floated in the international marketplace. The bonds, which were chiefly bought by European investors, paid 6 percent interest, payable in half-yearly installments in Amsterdam, London, and Paris. Besides being one of the lead banks to issue the bonds, Barings of London had an even larger role. Like a globalized investment bank of today such as Goldman Sachs, Barings sent Alexander Barings, one of the bank's partners, to help the French and American negotiators structure the ultimate deal. Seventy years later the same Barings firm, along with Drexel Morgan, would again be involved with the American government in handling the refinancing of $300 million in Civil War debt.

By the time the Louisiana Purchase was completed, approximately 56 percent of the U.S. federal government debt was held abroad. At the same time, foreign investors also held 62 percent of the stock of the Bank of the United States, plus large minority holdings in the various state banks. The flow of international investment funds into the United States in the early 1800s was just a small taste of what was to come. Most economic historians consider the period from 1870 to the First World War as a precursor to our current era of globalization, and there is no better example of this than European-led investments into the emerging market of that time, the United States. The great American industrial revolution of that period was spurred by entrepreneurs such as Carnegie, Fiske, Stamford, Hill, Vanderbilt, and Harriman and built mostly with immigrant labor. But the funds that enabled the building of those railroads, steel mills, and electric generators, and that financed the raw materials for these new factories, came mostly from foreign investors.

The United States between 1860 and 1900 was the embodiment of globalization, with nearly twelve million new immigrants supplying labor for its new factories, and significant foreign funds supplying capital for these factories. In the decades following the American Civil War, foreign funds coming into the United States resembled a metaphorical tsunami. Between 1861 and 1875 foreign investors rushed into the United States at unprecedented levels, lending just under $1.5 billion (approximately $32 billion in today's economy). After 1875 there was a small respite, but the inflow of foreign investment continued expanding rapidly in the fourteen years from 1882 to 1896. The new investments totaled more than $1.7 billion, a figure that exceeds the earlier one by more than a quarter of a billion dollars.

From the 1860s through the 1890s, American railroads were analogous to the internet of today, the new dynamic technology that changed how people interacted. The shareholders of these new engines of growth, however, were globalized at a level far surpassing foreign shareholding in American tech giants of the early twenty-first century. By 1890 foreign investors—primarily from Great Britain, the Netherlands, Germany, and France—held 50–75 percent of the equity in the famous Pennsylvania Railroad, the New York Railroad, the Louisville and Nashville Railroad, the Illinois Central, and the Philadelphia and Reading Railroads. They also owned more than one-fifth of the stock of the Great Northern, the Baltimore and Ohio, and the Chicago, Milwaukee, and Saint Paul Railroad. And Barings Bank of London, of Louisiana Purchase fame, was involved in the public issue of the legendary Atchison, Topeka, and Santa Fe Railroad. The amount of American railroad equity and debt traded on the London Stock Exchange at the time was so large that a section of the exchange was set aside for American rails.

Although the majority of foreign capital investment in the United States at that time went into railroads, substantial funds also went into other industries such as mining, agriculture, and the emerging manufacturing sector. By 1914 a quarter of the shares of U.S. Steel were held abroad. There was also a slew of what we would call today vcs—venture capital firms—set up in the Netherlands, Great Britain, and France, that invested in all sorts of merging American companies, from meatpackers to breweries. And similar to the situation today, as the world's largest recipient of foreign capital, the United States was the world's largest "debtor nation." This status meant that even in its period of most rapid economic growth, the United States had larger obligations to foreigners than foreigners had to it.

What was particularly different about the American experience in the pre–World War I era of globalization vis-à-vis other areas of the world at that time was that the United States was not part of any major colonial bloc. Although world trade was extensive during that period—in fact, it took until the mid-1980s to reach the levels of global trade that had taken place in the years before World War I—most of that trade was within the various imperial or colonial blocks. For example, the United Kingdom traded heavily with its colony India, and France with its colony Indochina. While trade within colonial networks boomed, the trade between the Great Powers—Germany and the United Kingdom, for example—was limited. By not being part of a prefixed colonial trade group, the United States was in the unique position of being able to freely trade with and borrow money from all and benefited by being open to all comers. This unique status was also true in another area of globalization: immigration.

Few people epitomize American globalization of the post–Civil War era more than the financier J. P. Morgan. Morgan is famous as the man who consolidated the U.S. railroad industry, founded U.S. Steel as well as General Electric, and was one of the forefathers of the bank we know today as JPMorgan Chase. But Morgan was much more than that. He was America's first true "Davos Man," financing projects around the world and friendly with the British royalty, the German kaiser, and various other foreign leaders. And Morgan's first truly big success came by acting as the main broker between the new American industries that needed capital to grow and investors in Europe who had the capital.

Morgan was the son of a New England merchant who had moved to London to join the American George Peabody in merchant banking. He was educated in Boston and at the University of Gottingen in Germany, where he learned to speak German proficiently. Both his father's London connections and his early experiences on the European continent would later become important in his role as the nineteenth-century version of the globalized investment banker.

In 1871 Morgan became a partner in the New York City firm of Drexel, Morgan, and Company. In this ideal business marriage, Drexel had relationships with the newly industrializing Pennsylvania entrepreneurs who needed funding, while Morgan—through his London relationship—was able to sell what were then called trade credits (a manner of financing raw material at that time) of these new industries to clients in London. Drexel benefited by having access to Morgan's investors, while Morgan benefited by having products to sell to European investors. In the following years J. P. Morgan became the go-to person for connecting European investors to the new, capital-hungry American industries.

While we think of J. P. Morgan as an American financier, his world was the globalized marketplace of the time. In the transaction that would crown Morgan as the king of Wall Street, William Vanderbilt—the majority shareholder of the New York Central Railroad—asked Morgan to sell his controlling shares in the railroad without driving down the share price. The deal, which represented the largest sale of stock ever publicly offered at that time, could not have taken place without Morgan's European connections. The sale was done by Morgan in Europe, primarily in London, where it was handled with such finesse that the share price remained even. Besides earning a fee of $3 million (approximately $70 million in today's dollars) for the transaction, Morgan received a seat on the New York Central's board, representing the English investors.

During the following years, with his knowledge of German, Morgan developed a strong relationship with the newly created Deutsche Bank. With that bank as a syndicate partner, he put together financing for the Northern Pacific Railroad in the United States. He also worked with Deutsche Bank in financing the Cataract Construction Company, which developed hydroelectricity at Niagara Falls in 1890, and a Mexican sovereign debt issue in 1898.

With the combination of foreign capital flowing into the United States through Morgan and others, massive immigration providing pools of cheap labor, a land rich in raw materials, and bountiful agriculture, the economy of the United States became the largest in the world by the beginning of the twentieth century. This mixture of attributes was so fortuitous that the living standards of U.S. citizens was surpassing anything the world had ever known. Per-capita American incomes at the time were double those of Germany and France and were 50 percent higher than Great Britain's. The United States had truly become the golden land.

The United States had two other advantages that made it a poster child for pre–World War I globalization: one, the rule of law and a stable government, and two, the English language. Rule of law and governmental stability were and are a key hedge in offsetting some of emerging market risk. And with the United Kingdom being the dominant power of the time, it of course was a benefit that business in the United States was done in English. These advantages continue to reverberate today. According to the United Nations Global Investment Trends model, the United States received approximately $251.814 billion in foreign direct investment (FDI) in 2018, while China as a comparison received approximately $139.043 trillion of FDI in 2018. And the A. T. Kearney FDI confidence index for 2019 again has the United States as the most confident place for foreign investment.

International investments and trade flows, however, comprise only the first half of any modern definition of globalization. Those words are always followed by statements such as "globalization is also an interaction and integration among the people," or as the World Economic Forum added to its definition, "a key component of today's globalization is a cultural element where traditions are traded and assimilated." And here again, although not always easily, this definition of globalization is part of the American birthright. Cultural integration is so much a part of the American character that most of the time we don't even recognize it anymore. It is everywhere, from my one-year-old granddaughter learning to speak Spanish as well as English in her day care center in Oakland, California, to bagels becoming part of the mainstream American diet, to jazz—the singular American art form—with its roots in Africa and slave culture, to the politically conservative roots of the grandchildren and great-grandchildren of the Dutch Reformed settlers in Upper Michigan.

While foreign investors were vital in the eighteenth and nineteenth centuries for the birth, physical expansion, and industrial growth of the United States, the very nature of how the nation developed historically, culturally, and legally has made it the default winner of twenty-first-century globalization. Whereas J. P. Morgan, the globalized Davos Man of the nineteenth century, was born into an old New England family, the leaders of American globalization of the late twentieth century and early twenty-first are in many cases children of immigrants or immigrants themselves. The father of Apple's founder, Steve Jobs, was a Syrian immigrant, while the family of Sergey Brin, a co-founder of Google, emigrated from the Soviet Union when he was five years old. Andy Grove, one of the co-founders of Intel, came to the United States from Hungary when he was twenty, while Elon Musk, the founder of Tesla, immigrated to the United States from South Africa, and Dara Khosrowshahi, the CEO of Uber, came to the United States from Iran as a child.

Even those who are not immigrants themselves are frequently immediate descendants of immigrants, such as Jamie Dimon, whose grandparents came from Greece and who now occupies a globalized banking role similar to that of Morgan, ironically at Morgan's namesake institution JPMorgan Chase. Today, immigrants or close descendants of immigrants make up a large preponderance of America's globalized leaders.

America's historic tradition of immigration and cultural integration, combined with the clash of ideas that is inherent in the integration process, has given the United States a distinct comparative advantage in the current age of globalization. In an era where ideas are money, it is this blend of diverse thought and multiculturalism that acts as America's catalyst for creativity—and prosperity.

Historically of course America's cultural integration was anathema to ideologies that feared the mixture of people. It is not surprising that a theme running through Nazi propaganda in the 1930s was that America's cultural assimilation created what Hitler labeled a "mongrel nation made up of a mongrel people." Hitler and his propaganda chief, Goebbels, mocked the United States for its mixture of races and cultures, which they believed prevented America from achieving the height of European culture as interpreted by the Nazis.

But putting aside for the moment how sick, demented, and evil the Nazis' perception of the world was, it is ironic that what the Nazis, and even some in the contemporary United States, labeled degenerate, being a "mongrel nation" is one of the keys to why America will continue to dominate globalization. It is one of the United States' major comparative advantages.

David Ricardo, the great British economist, formulated the theory of comparative advantage in 1817. While Ricardo obviously had no understanding of the technology-based world of today, the definition of comparative advantage, the ability of any given economic actor to produce goods and services at a lower opportunity cost, that is, more efficiently than others, still holds. The United States is the global leader in technology because it creates it more efficiently. Unlike the construction of railroads and steel mills in the nineteenth century, when the keys to efficiency were the ready availability of capital, inexpensive labor, and the supply of raw materials, today the key ingredient is the free flow and ferment of ideas within a society. This ferment of ideas is one of the keys that enable America to be the global leader in technology.

Globalization, technology, and the integration of global manufacturing and supply lines have radically changed the values that are used to measure nations' underlying economic health and well-being. In the nineteenth and twentieth centuries it was common to measure a country's wealth by its steel production, auto production, and the amount of railroad track laid. For example, the United Kingdom began to feel threatened in the early 1900s when German steel production surpassed that of Britain's. And a key to both Stalin's and Mao's famous five-year plans was ever-increasing steel production. Today a nation's wealth is increasingly measured not in fixed assets like steel mills but in human capital.

That is why China's leaders in the twenty-first century are no longer bragging about steel production but instead are struggling to replicate Silicon Valley within the framework of a semi-state-controlled economy. And Vladimir Putin stated that the nation that leads in artificial intelligence, or AI, will be the ruler of the world. The problem, of course, is that it is relatively easy to produce steel under state direction. Steel mills are producing an industrial product whose patterns for production are set up by strict guidelines. The generation of ideas, on the other hand, is a very different matter.

The concept of the state-controlled economy directly conflicts with the software engineer who can create an idea and translate it into an algorithm, or the entrepreneur who understands almost instinctively how to exploit the engineer's ideas, or the venture capitalist who judges financially which ideas will be attractive and which will not.

Three primary cultural and historic patterns give the United States a distinct advantage over other countries. First of these is cultural assimilation, which I mentioned earlier. Second is that the United States is one of the few countries whose government and constitution were based on the philosophy of the eighteenth-century age of Enlightenment in Europe.

Part of the Enlightenment philosophy stressed the rights of the individual over that of government. America's founders revolted against the idea of a king or queen or sovereign having the responsibility for the nation. Thomas Jefferson, a true son of the Enlightenment, clearly wrote in the Declaration of Independence, "That to secure these rights [life, liberty and the pursuit of happiness], Governments are instituted among Men." In the eyes of its founders, the American government was being created not to watch over the individual welfare of its citizens but to guarantee their fundamental rights to liberties.

In Europe, China, and Japan modern government has been derived from the historic tradition of the king or queen or emperor, the sovereigns being responsible for their subjects. Of course in Europe and Japan today the rights of the individual are insured constitutionally, but in part due to the tradition of monarchism, the responsibility of the government to its citizens' well-being is dramatically broader than in the United States. Just look at what appears to be the never-ending political health care fights in the U.S. and consider why the United States of all the modern economies lacks universal health care. The answer goes directly back to the Enlightenment idea of the rights of the individual, and the limits of the role of government.

Although the fact that the United States was born with the rights of the individual as part of its mother's milk gives it a schizophrenic health care system, that same Enlightenment nourishment has helped enable its tech industry to dominate the globalized world. Because of the perceived limited role of government in the United States versus that of other countries, two related concepts—creative disruption, observed by the Austrian economist Joseph Shumpeter, and disruptive innovation, by the Harvard professor Clayton Christensen—could essentially merge in the United States and allow tech companies to invent new way of doing things without worrying that the government would interfere to protect established workers or industries that might be disrupted in the process. As an example, it would be very strange within American culture if the government protected printing houses against the Kindle or research librarians against Google.

Shumpeter's creative disruption outlines how economic progress is not gradual or peaceful but rather disjointed and possibly unpleasant. Whenever an entrepreneur disrupts an existing industry, it is likely that existing workers, businesses, or even entire sectors can be temporarily thrown into disarray. Christensen's idea of disruptive innovation refers to an innovation that creates a new market and value network and eventually disrupts an existing market and value network, displacing established market-leading firms and products. Schumpeter was writing about nations and cultures, while Christensen was addressing companies and industries. Examples of Christensen's concept are Uber's disruption of the taxi industry, Airbnb's effect on the hotel industry, Wikipedia destroying the encyclopedia industry, and iPhones disrupting landlines as well as the photography and film industries. And in an open dynamic economy like that of the United States, this process never ends. In 2017 Uber was only eight years old, yet a new company Via was already disrupting the Uber pricing model in major U.S. cities.

Neither Schumpeter's nor Christensen's concepts are illogical, although they can be unsettling to established cultural patterns. In the United States, however, by tradition and by law these concepts are given free reign. By comparison, in Europe, the sovereign (government) generally sees as its right and its duty the protection of its "vassals" from destruction, that is, maintaining balance within the society.

In a wonderful and still relevant piece titled "Why Germans Are Afraid of Google" in the *New York Times* on October 10, 2014, Anna Sauerbrey sums up this difference between America and Europe perfectly, clearly outlining what Europeans see as the "libertarian cowboy, anything goes" American culture and the more state-focused culture of Europe.

> Germany is known for being many things: a leader in clean technology, a manufacturing powerhouse, Europe's foreign policy center. But increasingly, it seems to have taken on yet another stereotype—as a nation of Luddites.
>
> Germany is not a great place to be a big tech company these days.
>
> Google is often spoken of in dark terms. People regularly call it the Octopus.

30

Google isn't the only target of Teutonic ire. A few weeks ago, a German court prohibited Uber from operating in the country, reasoning that the company was violating federal licensing laws for drivers. And Amazon is entangled in a long and wearying battle over working conditions and pay.

To outsiders, this all seems like just another instance of collective German angst. But Germans don't fear technology. In politics, Silicon Valley is a magic phrase. It's what Berlin wants to be.

What gives? How can Germany be both afraid of and in love with technology, and the companies that make it?

The true origin of the conflict lies in the economic culture innate to those Silicon Valley giants. To create and grow Amazon or Uber takes a certain cowboy mind-set that ignores obstacles and rules.

Silicon Valley fears neither fines nor political reprimand. It finds the [European] democratic political process too slow. Uber simply declared that it would keep operating in Germany, no matter what the courts ruled. Amazon is pushing German publishers to offer their books on its platform at a lower price—ignoring that, in Germany, publishers are legally required to offer their books at the same price everywhere.

It is this anarchical spirit that makes Germans so neurotic. On one hand, we'd love to be more like that: more daring, more aggressive. On the other hand, the force of anarchy makes Germans shudder.

What Sauerbrey didn't discuss was that the so-called American libertarian culture offers a tremendous advantage to American companies. With basically no limits on how disruptive innovation migrates through the marketplace, America's most innovative companies have a built-in incubator and test market of 326 million people for their products. And because of the merger between technology and globalization, products that have been successfully test-driven in the American marketplace can then immediately go globally viral.

Being a cultural child of the Enlightenment has given America a tremendous comparative advantage in our age of globalization,

31

but this philosophical heritage sadly has had a disquieting down-side. Simply put, when there is extreme economic dislocation in America—whether it is because of globalization or the combination of automation and artificial intelligence or a myriad of other reasons—there is not an automatic government response to try to ameliorate these problems. Instead they are left to fester in a nowhere land of political and philosophical debate. One would have thought that Franklin Roosevelt had resolved this issue during the Great Depression. Unfortunately, however, the debate over the proper governmental response to economic dislocation continues and, in the process, feeds populism and nativism, as well as causing pain and hardship.

Despite the ubiquity of globalization in America, the mixed blessing of Enlightenment in American culture is the primary reason globalization is not celebrated politically, even though the United States has been the winner and will probably continue to be the winner in the game of globalization. I will discuss more about this in chapter 3.

The third advantage that the United States has over other countries is that it generally adheres to four guiding principles that allow human capital to thrive. These are:

1. Guarantee the rule of law over the rule of personality, group, ideology, or vested interest. On August 10, 2017, the *New York Times* had a front-page story titled "Russia Wants Innovation, but It's Arresting Its Innovators," by Andrew Higgins. If there was ever a story that clearly demonstrates the rule of law over the rule of personality for the development of a tech sector, it is this one.

The article is about how Dmitri Trubitsyn, a young physicist-entrepreneur, was put under house arrest on August 3, 2017, simply because his company, Tion, manufactures innovative high-tech air-purification systems for homes and hospitals. He and his company were accused of risking the lives of hospital patients, and trying to lift profits, by upgrading the purifiers so they would consume less electricity.

Most important, he was accused of doing this without state regulators certifying the changes.

Andrew Higgins explains:

Using a 2014 law meant to protect Russians from counterfeit medicine, investigators from the Federal Security Service, the post-Soviet KGB, and other agencies have accused Mr. Trubitsyn of leading a criminal conspiracy to, essentially, innovate too fast and too freely.

Natalia Pinus, Akademgorodok's elected representative to the regional council, is one of many local residents who see Mr. Trubitsyn's troubles as the fault of unscrupulous operators able to manipulate law-enforcement agencies to wipe out competitors.

"This is not just about a single company," she said, but "whether you can conduct honest business in Russia or whether that is impossible."

Police raids and arrests figure prominently in many Russian business struggles, particularly those involving assets like oil, over which the state has steadily reasserted control under Mr. Putin. Private companies that clash with Rosneft, Russia's state-owned energy giant, for example, often face criminal investigation.

The decline in global oil prices has, however, also meant less money is available for siphoning by venal officials. That has turned even relatively small companies into attractive targets by the police and the courts operating in partnership with business.

Anton Latkin, a computer programmer who has known Mr. Trubitsyn since boyhood science clubs, said Tion had fallen prey to attack by government officials who "don't understand anything about physics, don't understand anything about chemistry and don't understand anything about biology."

Mr. Amelkin, Tion's chief technical officer, said he and his staff had been unable to figure out who or what was behind the investigation. "If you try to find out who is responsible for anything in this system, you will only find an echo in the cave," he said, adding that the Russian state "is not a single organism with one brain" but a sprawling mass of separate and often competing fiefs.

2. The second principle is bifurcated in that knowledge must be

open and transferable, while at the same time the rights to an idea must be protected.

This is extremely important but a strange duality, which at first glance appears to be almost contradictory. But it is not. Most great ideas are a synthesis of various concepts, a give-and-take among individuals that then spurs a new original idea. This second principle is about allowing the freedom—either culturally or legally—for the back-and-forth to occur, and then legally protecting through copyright the new concept so that its creator can be rewarded for it.

The importance to the growth of a technology industry of the concept of knowledge being open and transferable becomes apparent when you look at the cultural and strangely the legal history of that industry in the United States. The tech industry originally grew up in the Boston area around Route 128 near Harvard University and the Massachusetts Institute of Technology (MIT). In fact, a Pulitzer Prize–winning book, *The Soul of a New Machine*, written by Tracy Kidder and published in 1981, described the growth and culture of the new computer industry as it grew in the Boston area.

But then something happened, and today the home of American technology is not between Harvard and MIT in Massachusetts but between Stanford and Berkeley in California. So why did it move? While California's weather is better than the weather of New England, that difference couldn't have been the sole motivation. AnnaLee Saxenian, dean of the University of California, Berkeley, School of Information, in her groundbreaking 1994 book *Regional Advantage: Culture and Competition in Silicon Valley and Route 128*, explains that the key was Silicon Valley's decentralized organizational form, a tradition of exchanging ideas among engineers from different companies (sharing information and outsourcing for component parts), as opposed to a more closed hierarchic corporate environment in the Boston area. Essentially, engineers from various companies in Silicon Valley could and would meet at Starbucks for coffee in the morning or at their kids' sports game and go over an idea or a problem, a phenomenon that did not happen in the more structured, traditional corporate environment of

Boston. In Silicon Valley, companies compete intensely with each other while also learning from each other.

Besides the schmoozing at Starbucks, most economic historians believe that a small but vital legal issue also helped spur the move of the computer industry to California. Massachusetts's law allowed noncompete clauses in employee contracts, while California law did not. A noncompete clause in a contract between the employee and the corporation prevents the employee, if they leave the company, from working for a competitor for a specific time. This small difference in California law fostered a much more footloose engineer-as-employee base in Silicon Valley, where engineers could and can easily move from company to company, thus cross-fertilizing development.

The second half of the principle, that the rights to an idea must be protected, is not only a common part of the Silicon Valley culture; one could even speculate that it would be impossible to have developed a modern technology industry without the concept of copyrights and legal protection of one's ideas.

Trademarks and copyright protection are not a new concept, but the enforcement of copyrights—or allowing them to happen in the first place—has had an amazing effect historically on global economic development and competitiveness. In her wonderful book *The Travels of a T-shirt in the Global Economy*, Pietra Rivoli uses Eli Whitney and his invention of the cotton gin in 1793 as an example that clearly shows how important these laws are.

Rivoli explains how even with slavery in the U.S., American cotton growing outside the South Carolina coast in the latter part of the eighteenth century was not profitable on the global market, because of the time needed to pick out all the seeds. Then along came Eli Whitney with his patented invention, the cotton gin, a machine that picked the seeds out of the ball of cotton. As Rivoli explains, with Whitney's invention cotton production rose twenty-five-fold over the next eight years, and more than ninetyfold by 1820. And of course because Whitney had a patent on his cotton gin he and his investor were able to benefit from the idea.

The question Rivoli asks is, If the production of cotton exploded in the United States after the invention of the cotton gin, why couldn't the traditional growing areas in Asia compete and why was there no Eli Whitney in China? As she explains,

> First, there were no property rights, there were no incentives to improve age-old methods, to learn, to grow more, to do better. In China, cotton growers would not have benefited. Under the tyranny of the emperor, there was little reason to take a business risk in the modern sense of the term. As a Christian missionary remarked in the late 1700s, "Any man of genius is paralyzed immediately by the thought that his efforts will win him punishment rather than rewards." China's "cultural triumphalism [at that time] and petty downward tyranny made [the country] a reluctant improver and a bad learner." A Jesuit passing through commented that the Chinese were "more fond of the most defective piece of antiquity than of the most perfect of the modern." In other words, all of the Elis in China had no reason to try.

3. The third principle is obvious: insure peace and tranquility. Make a place safe for the engineer and the technological entrepreneur to live.

4. The fourth and last principle is that a country needs to have a private and transparent venture capital system that will make investments—and reap the benefits from those investments—based on the value of the project, not on whether the project is politically well connected. The importance of this point cannot be understated. When the state interferes through political cronyism and forces investments to go to friends or for political expediency, instead of to what could be the best idea, the damage to economic progress and efficiency is obvious.

The ability to adhere to these four principles, along with the dynamics of multiculturalism and America's so-called libertarian culture, gives the United States a unique comparative advantage as the current age of globalization moves from being driven by labor and capital to being driven by capital and knowledge. Think about it: What other country or area of the world has this combination of cultural skill sets?

Europe comes closest, but then, as we have seen, it lacks the cowboy culture of experimentalism and of course the multicultural mix. The Chinese, who are investing substantial funds into technological research, will lag because they fear the free exchange of ideas, see disruption as a negative, and are plagued by political cronyism in investments. Russia isn't even in the game. Of the four principles I mentioned, Russia can deliver only on one, the insurance of peace and tranquility. Besides the issues of corruption, disregard for the rule of law, and no guarantee of rights to an idea, the Russian government believes you can duplicate Silicon Valley by building a city and throwing engineers into it; they don't understand it is a combination of culture and rule of law that creates Silicon Valley, rather than simply assembling groups of engineers in a room. And then there is Japan, with its keiretsu-conglomerate-like corporate structure, where very large firms control smaller firms. This system was ideal during the age of manufacturing, but now the top-down manufacturing structure of the keiretsu limits innovation from the ground up.

There is one other major area that gives the United States a comparative advantage in the age of globalization. As the largest open market in the world, the United States allows American companies to learn how to compete in the global market at home. This advantage seems like a simple thing, but it is very important. Apple learns how to compete against Samsung on Apple's turf before it takes its products overseas. With various exclusions of America's most advanced tech companies in China, the Chinese companies do not have this advantage. They grow and prosper in a protective state system, in an almost monopolistic environment, and as a result are ill-prepared for the street fight in the globalized world. The same problem also applies to the homogeneous management of the Chinese, Japanese, or Russian company that prevents it from understanding other cultures. Here again America's multiculturalism and its more diverse corporate leadership are a distinct advantage, enabling Americans to see the world more broadly.

On March 9, 2016, Warren Buffett stated, "For 240 years it's been a terrible mistake to bet against America, and now is no time to start.

America's golden goose of commerce and innovation will continue to lay more and larger eggs. America's social security promises will be honored and perhaps made more generous. And, yes, America's kids will live far better than their parents did."

One major caveat to Buffett's statement exists, however: Does America have the political wherewithal and agility to allow itself to continue to be the winner of globalization? Will we realize that globalization is our game to lose? Or will the political conflict inherent in our governing system, exasperated by the rapid economic changes brought on by twenty-first-century globalization, force the United States into retreat from globalization?

In the next chapter, we will look at those forces arrayed against a globalized United States both internally and externally—what I call the counterrevolution against globalization—and examine why they will fail.

TWO

"Make It Like It Was"

I t is an irrefutable fact that one cannot win a war that is already lost. Globalization has captured and taken control of the American economy, just as the automobile did in the first half of the twentieth century; there is no going back. The counterrevolution against globalization—represented by Trump and his supporters—may have won the election in 2016, but the election was a victory of perception, not reality. In actuality, the revolt against globalization has already lost the war.

Put aside the number of sushi or Indian restaurants in Wichita, Kansas, or the percentage of non-Americans now playing professional sports in the United States. When it comes to jobs and the economy it is no longer possible to "deglobalize" America. The number of employed people in the United States in 2019 was approximately 132,160,000 people. Trade Partnership Worldwide, LLC, estimated in 2018 that the number of U.S. jobs depending on trade, that is, U.S. exports and imports of goods and services, totaled around 36 million, or more than a quarter of all the jobs in the country. And in fact trade-related jobs grew almost four times as fast as non-trade-related jobs during the past twenty-four years.

Ironically, manufacturing—so often portrayed as a victim of globalization—had the highest level of jobs dependent on exports. Moreover, for every job within manufacturing supported by the export of manufactured products, there is also a job supported in service industries by the export of those manufactured products.

While thirty-six million jobs related to the export or import of goods and services is a huge number in its own right, it includes only trade-related jobs, not jobs dependent on another facet of globalization: foreign direct investment (FDI). FDI would comprise jobs in the United States based on foreign plant ownership: for example, the Toyota factory in Blue Springs, Mississippi. According to the International Trade Administration of the U.S. government, twelve million people, or 9 percent of the labor force, have jobs in the U.S. due to direct employment at foreign firms.

Ultimately, of a total American workforce of nearly 132,160,000 people, forty-eight million, or 36 percent of the workforce, have jobs tied to globalization. To put this number in perspective, compare it with the approximately 22,300,000 people working for local, state, or federal governments in the United States in 2018, or the approximately 16,866,000 people who worked in health care.

Of the forty-eight million people in the United States whose jobs are tied to globalization, approximately sixteen million of them work in jobs related to importing products into the United States. Economically, globalization describes the flow of goods freely around the world, both exports and imports. So whether it is the sixty thousand people working at importing steel or all of Walmart's retail workers and warehouse employees, the importing part of globalization is a major job creator in the United States as well. Adding to the economic importance of imports is the fact that distribution and marketing are now bigger profit generators than manufacturing, and as automation increases in manufacturing, imports will be bigger job creators.

Imports are the stealth economic stimulus, politically difficult to defend because they are seen perversely as job destroyers, not job creators. And of course they put pricing pressure and also innovative pressure on American industry. But the value of imports to the U.S. economy goes far beyond the sixteen million jobs that are involved. Taken as a whole, imports have a huge "multiplier effect" on the wider economy. The multiplier effect is an increase in spending causing an increase in consumption much greater than the initial money spent.

Besides being a check on inflation, and forcing American industry to be more competitive both in pricing and quality—for example, the U.S. auto industry was forced to improve its quality standards when they were confronted by Japanese car imports in the 1970s and 1980s—imports directly stimulate the economy by putting more funds into the hands of consumers. Consider the amount of spending, or economic demand, that would be taken out of the economy if the average citizen had to pay almost three times more for a basic item like jeans.

The word *imports*, however, despite its positive association with the U.S. economy, is a pejorative in American politics. Politically, imports represent the loss of manufacturing jobs in the United States. Even when imports are directly beneficial to manufacturing jobs as when companies utilize a globally integrated supply chain to bring various components from around the world into the United States to make the finished product cheaper and more competitive, for the sake of their careers, politicians will not mention the benefits of imports. But those benefits quietly exist in economic data, and in consumer preferences.

Of course, the political argument against imports ignores the real culprits in the loss of manufacturing jobs, technology and automation. The steel industry is perhaps the best example. In the late 1970s, it took ten workers to make a ton of steel, while today it takes only one. And this change in the steel industry is just a reflection of an economic evolutionary change that is happening as the world rapidly moves out of the industrial age and into the age of human capital. Essentially, the value of manufacturing is falling globally and manufacturing no longer represents the essence of a nation's wealth.

Jagdish Bhagwati, a noted economist at Columbia University, argues that "those who argue in favour of boosting rich-world manufacturing suffer from a 'manufacturing fetish.'" One reason for the fascination with manufacturing, Bhagwati says, "is the mistaken belief that it is more technologically dynamic than service industries." He points, however, to logistics companies, major retailers, and mobile telecommunications as sources of innovation in non-financial services, and to genetically modified seeds as the most prominent example in agriculture.

To Bhagwati, the idea that domestic manufacturing is a better for job creation

> is fundamentally flawed. Changing the composition of output in favour of manufacturing industries especially in wealthier countries is not critical for job creation.
>
> As emerging economies become richer, they will want more of all sorts of services, including sophisticated ones where countries like America and Britain retain a comparative advantage. Those who pitch for manufacturing on the ground that it is better at boosting exports often ignore the fact that an increasing number of services are traded, and that rich countries tend to export more of them than they import. America and Britain, for instance, typically run surpluses in services.

An easy way to demonstrate how the antiglobalists have already lost the war both politically and economically is to look at one of their favorite anathemas and political stalking horses: the North Atlantic Free Trade Agreement, or NAFTA. When President Trump constantly harped on the evils and failure of NAFTA, he was seemingly unaware that NAFTA represents more than a quarter of the global economy. And possibly because of his political naivete and his oversimplification of issues, he failed to realize that NAFTA was like Obamacare in that everybody hated it until they tried to take it away.

The case for NAFTA was obvious. In the years since NAFTA was established, U.S. trade with its North American neighbors has more than tripled, growing more rapidly than U.S. trade with the rest of the world. Canada and Mexico are the two largest destinations for U.S. exports, accounting for more than a third of the total.

Where NAFTA has its greatest impact is on American agriculture. U.S. farm exports to Canada and Mexico grew 156 percent since the establishment of the agreement. That's compared with a 65 percent increase in farm exports to the rest of the world. Agricultural exports from the United States to Canada and Mexico alone were greater than exports to the next six largest markets combined. Mexico is the top export destination for U.S. beef, rice, soybean meal, corn sweeteners, apples, and beans. It is the second-largest export destination for corn, soybeans, and oils. Mexico is the second-largest market for farm products from Colorado, and it makes up 19.2 percent of Nebraska's foreign trade at a value of $1.26 billion. Politically, for the agricultural states, NAFTA had become like the old World War I song, "How Ya Gonna Keep 'Em Down on the Farm After They've Seen Paree" with revised lyrics to read, "How Ya Gonna Keep 'Em as Antiglobalist Once They've Seen NAFTA."

For large-scale manufacturing industries in the United States, NAFTA has been also equally important, although because of globalized integrated supply chains the data is not as obvious as it is with agriculture. One of the underlying purposes of NAFTA was to create a trade bloc that in size could compete with the European Union and China. In theory, it was a natural combination, linking the capital and manufacturing in the United States with the natural resources of Canada and the labor pool in Mexico. Of course, converting theory into reality doesn't happen overnight, especially while challenging preexisting trade patterns, cultural differences, and massive shifts in where factory investments should be made. But with the relatively new concept of international integrated supply lines—mixing parts and production wherever they are made or done more efficiently in the world, NAFTA has been a major force in modernizing the U.S. auto industry by consolidating manufacturing and driving down costs. Most cars made in North America now have parts sourced from all three countries. The integrated auto supply line between the United States, Mexico, and Canada has created another interesting phenomenon that demonstrates the interconnectedness of globalization. The absolute value of the U.S. component of parts assembled in Mexico and shipped to the United States for placement in larger products has more than tripled since 1995 to almost $40 billion by 2014, the year of the latest figures.

NAFTA has enabled manufacturers such as General Motors to create a seamless supply chain so that the company can make inexpensive products in Mexico and manufacture its more expensive value-added products in the U.S. or Canada. This arrangement allows GM to be much more competitive against imports from Asia, in particular, by enabling it to increase the scale of production and averaging costs.

The integrated seamless supply chain for auto manufacturing is not unique to North America; globally, every major auto-producing economy uses it, to make their products more competitive. In Europe, German and French automobile parts are outsourced to central Europe to assure competitiveness. In Asia, Japan relies on joint production with Thailand and other southeast Asian countries to continue expanding its global presence. In North America—and specifically in the United States—employment is actually growing in the automobile industry, thanks to integrated supply chains. From 2009 to 2016, manufacturing jobs in motor vehicles and auto parts in the United States grew by 276,000, or 41.6 percent, according to the Bureau of Labor Statistics. Notably, this increase occurred while Mexico also expanded in terms of capacity and penetration in the regional market.

As in the case of Obamacare, Donald Trump was not able to do away with NAFTA. After attacking it for two years, he signed a new NAFTA treaty on October 1, 2018. Of course he gave it a new name, USMCA so he could say that NAFTA no longer exists. But in reality USMCA is almost identical to the old NAFTA except for some reworded updates borrowed from the Trans-Pacific Partnership agreement that the Obama administration had negotiated and which Trump refused to pursue.

If being unable to win a war already lost is the first reason why the counterrevolution against globalization will fail, the second reason is another irrefutable fact: you can't bring back yesterday. America today is richer than it has ever been and is in the healthiest condition of any major global economy, yet many Americans don't see it that way. Like Ed Koch's elderly constituent that I mentioned in the introduction, many want it to be like it "used to be." Trying to bring back yesterday—whether due to current economic hardship and fear of the future or because of pleasant memories and nostalgia—is part of the human political condition, no matter how impossible it may be. References to it are even in the Bible: the Israelites rebelled against Moses and the future and wanted to return to slavery and the perceived safety of Egypt.

In many ways the fight against globalization is all about "making it like it used to be." Consider America's small cities, once the prosperous definition of America but which are now culturally, politically, and economically unsuited to survive the changes brought about by globalization and the information economy.

As Eduardo Porter pointed out in the *New York Times* on October 10, 2017,

By now, most Americans live in big metropolitan clusters. Still, the stagnation of small cities is hardly inconsequential.

Yet it is unclear what should be done to slow the decline of small-city America. For what is driving the decline is the flip side of the forces powering the success of large metropolises: the accumulation of human talent that is spurring investment and driving innovations that are fueling the prosperity of the nation as a whole.

Some of the advantages of big-city living are not hard to find. For starters, big cities have a greater variety of employers and thus more job opportunities in a richer mix of industries than do small cities, whose fortunes are often tied to those of just a small number of employers.

Bigger cities are more productive. They are more innovative. They draw better-educated workers by offering them higher wages. They develop a richer variety of industries. It should not be surprising that they are growing faster.

It was not always so. In the decades after World War II, the share of jobs in big metropolitan areas actually declined, as employment growth spread to smaller cities.

But that was a different economy. Unlike with manufacturing, which took root in cities large and small, and in exurban industrial parks, opportunity in the information era has clustered in dense urban enclaves where high-tech businesses can tap into rich pools of skilled and creative people.

"The thickness of a labor market is crucial in the innovation industries that are drivers of economic success today," said Enrico Moretti, an economist at the University of California, Berkeley. "This applies to the biotech engineer but not to the welder, who has more replaceable skills."

In these small cities, it is just not the retirees wishing for the past world that they were more familiar with; it is the reality of empty storefronts, and the brain drain of young people leaving for Chicago, New York, or San Francisco.

When manufacturing was king, there was an economic reason for smaller cities to prosper, but sadly that economic world was yesterday; in the modern information economy, that model is impossible to go back to. For example, consider all the people who used to make cameras and film for Kodak in upstate New York; does anyone buy a Brownie camera or film anymore? These small American cities voted overwhelmingly for Trump over Clinton in the 2016 American presidential election—57 percent to 38 percent—and it is not difficult to understand why.

In addition to what the residents of small cities see all around them is the hard-to-understand but easily exploitable fact that global economics is not a zero-sum game. These people constantly see and hear stories about how wealthy China has become and compare those news items with the decline in their own neighborhoods and cities. But what appears to be obvious—that if another country has grown wealthier, your country is now poorer—is just not so. World economic growth is not like a ball game: the supposed winning team does not win because the home team lost. In this sense, world economic growth is counterintuitive.

China has become significantly wealthier over the past forty years, as we all know, but so has the United States. While the U.S. economy more than doubled during that period, China's grew at a much higher rate, but it had much more room to grow. The point is that the United States did not get poorer as China grew—quite the opposite.

Compounding the illusion that if China got richer the United States had to get poorer is the false view that just because the U.S. economy is no longer globally dominant, the United States has lost out. In 1945 the United States economy represented approximately 50 percent of the world's gross domestic product, substantially greater than its amount of 25 percent in 2016. Once again, these figures mean not that the United States has gotten poorer but that the rest of the world has fortunately grown wealthier. Europe in 1945, with its bombed-out factories and cities, was a pale shadow of the peaceful and prosperous European Union of today, and of course the same goes for China and Japan. It is not only totally logical that as the global economic pie got bigger the United States' portion of it—in percentage terms—would shrink, but it is also geopolitically better for the United States to be part an economically healthier world.

Certainly, some people in small cities have lost their jobs to globalization. Yet this was the main factor ten to twenty years ago, not today. In the political game of perception, antiglobalists make globalization the simplistic scapegoat for most of the job losses happening currently in American manufacturing, by attacking outsourcing to China, Japan, and Mexico. As reported by Bloomberg two years ago, however, this accusation was not true then, nor is it now.

> The U.S. had become the second-most-competitive manufacturing location among the 25 largest manufacturing exporters worldwide. While that news is welcome, most of the lost U.S. manufacturing jobs in recent decades aren't coming back. In 1970, more than a quarter of U.S. employees worked in manufacturing. By 2010, only one in 10 did.
>
> The growth in imports from China had a role in that decline—contributing, perhaps to as much as one-quarter of the employment drop-off from 1991 to 2007, according to an analysis by David Autor and his colleagues at the Massachusetts Institute of Technology. But the U.S. jobs slide began well before China's rise as a manufacturing power. And manufacturing employment is falling almost everywhere, including in China. The phenomenon is driven by technology.

Technological changes, brought on by the growth of the internet and advances in automation and artificial intelligence (AI), are creating chaos in what used to be the blue-collar worker's road to a middle-class lifestyle in the United States. Companies that used to print newspapers and books are now facing severe competition from e-readers. And then there is the U.S. automobile industry. In 2018 the United States manufactured 10.98 million vehicles, almost double the quantity of the early 1950s, when there were no imports. Yet those 2018 production numbers were achieved with almost the same number of workers as in 1953: approximately 998,000. A key difference appears to be automation. In 2018, 53 percent of all industrial robots ordered in North America went to the automobile industry. Automation is hardly limited to manufacturing, however. The teenage sons and daughters of many Americans used to work as part-time checkout clerks in supermarkets, jobs that today are increasingly being taken by automatic scanners.

Rapidly declining employment in the coal industry is another example of technological change although politically climate change and now even China are being blamed. In a masterful but irrational readjustment of facts, Donald Trump once tweeted, "The concept of global warming was created by and for the Chinese in order to make U.S. manufacturing non-competitive."

The decline in employment in the coal industry is partly due to climate change, but the main culprit is innovation in energy production. Natural gas is not only cleaner but now, due to innovations in fracking, also much more competitive for use as an energy source in manufacturing. Coal, like Kodak's old Brownie camera, is being innovated out of business.

In 1960 Harvard professor Theodore Levitt wrote an essay in *Harvard Business Review* titled "Marketing Myopia." In it Levitt refers to the destruction of buggy whip industries due to the advent of the automobile. This analogy has now entered the economic lexicon. Although Levitt's point was that if the buggy whip manufacturers were attuned to their market, they would have understood and adjusted to change, for the employees there was a benefit in that change that does not exist today. The buggy whip employees found better jobs relatively easily in the rapidly growing automobile industry. The same could be said throughout that period in American history, when millions left farms for cities because they were able to find better jobs in various forms of manufacturing with relative ease. Change was not frightening then, because new industrial jobs replaced the old occupations.

The difference today isn't globalization alone; it is also that for many people, change looks frightening and not positive. In the age of human capital, industrialized economies—whether in the United States, Germany, Japan, or China—will rely less and less on manufacturing. The need for agility to go from factory work to the gig economy, or tech, or entrepreneurialism, or services, is much greater than it was to go from the buggy whip factory to the automobile factory.

Because *globalization* is a word that is very hard to clarify, it can easily be distorted into fitting the politically false narrative of "make it like it used to be." Globalization means so much more than the definitions I wrote about in the introduction and chapter 1. As a word, it fits into the category of "sui generis," the Latin phrase that means "in a class by itself, unique, or not like anything else." As a concept globalization predates the idea of independent states by many thousands of years, and from the beginning of history it has been in an ongoing struggle against tribalism. Today, globalization for some people directly threatens their concept of yesterday, of neighborhoods where everyone looked just like themselves, jobs that you had for life, and the United States as the singularly most powerful nation in the world.

Over the millennia, globalization as a concept has not changed. Certainly, during different periods in history different parts of the compound definition of *globalization*—whether trade, finance, or culture—have gone back and forth in their importance, but the basic concept remains the same.

What has changed is twofold. First and most important, globalization is no longer gradual. With the advent of web technology, globalization, with its take-no-prisoners social change, speeds across the world as if it were Napoleon marching through Europe, leaving the people who cannot adapt to it in politically and culturally bewildered disarray. Second, globalization now permeates all levels of society. In the last era of globalization, the years before World War I, globalization was a game for elites. John Maynard Keynes, the noted economist and Cambridge don, wrote at the time:

> But escape was possible, for any man of capacity or character at all exceeding the average, into the middle and upper classes, for

whom life offered, at a low cost and with the least trouble, conveniences, comforts, and amenities beyond the compass of the richest and most powerful monarchs of other ages. The inhabitant of London could order by telephone, sipping his morning tea in bed, the various products of the whole earth, in such quantity as he might see fit, and reasonably expect their early delivery upon his doorstep; he could at the same moment and by the same means adventure his wealth in the natural resources and new enterprises of any quarter of the world, and share, without exertion or even trouble, in their prospective fruits and advantages.

We need to keep in mind that the common definition for middle class at that time in England was a family that had at least one servant. Also in the sentence preceding the two I quoted above, Keynes stated, "The greater part of the population [in the United Kingdom], it is true, worked hard and lived at a low standard of comfort, yet were, to all appearances, reasonably contented with this lot." The reality, however, is that this greater population, if we put aside for a second Keynes's upper-class view of contentment among the lower classes, didn't share in Keynes's globalized world of abundance.

Besides the class issue and speed, two other points separate our age of globalization from that earlier period. Keynes's England did not suffer from manufacturing jobs going abroad, nor the threat of automation and AI. And of course Keynes's England was not facing a huge flow of immigrants that would have challenged perceived British cultural mores. In fact, the situation was quite the opposite: during the Victorian and Edwardian eras fifteen million emigrants left the United Kingdom, mainly to settle in the United States, Canada, and Australia.

The speed and depth of our current era of globalization is truly a revolution, destroying old ways of doing things, devastating old economic and cultural patterns, and forcing new ways on people who are not prepared for them. And historically, like many revolutions, globalization has ignited a counterrevolution against it, both in the United States and in other leading democracies. While elsewhere, in countries such as Russia, Turkey, and Poland, there is open warfare by the leadership against the entire concept of globalization, with the leaders of these countries using technology and coercion to significantly reinforce the fear of change and the fear of the other in order to retain power.

Counterrevolutions have historically emerged to protect the old order: as an example, Catholics against Protestants during the Reformation era, or monarchists opposing republicans in the later Enlightenment period. And as with any counterrevolution, the one against globalization represents a fight to preserve the old way of life against a perceived threat of change.

In the United States, the counterrevolution against globalization acts as if globalization were an alien force of invaders that had to be stopped, not recognizing the fact that globalization is synonymous with the United States. The revolt's operating doctrine appears to be based on the populist philosophy that the purity and economic well-being of the country must be protected against evil "alien" influences. The old concept of the singular sovereign nation facing off against invaders still stands, but this time the invaders are seen as being not in tanks but rather in money wire transfers, in immigration, in the idea that one's life was better yesterday. And in a manner similar to that in Russia, Poland, or Turkey, the counterrevolutionists against globalization in the United States purposely overemphasize nationalism. For if one is frightened or doesn't understand—or doesn't want to partake in—the changes that globalization is forcing on society, then the very idea of believing that your country is exceptional, special, for a time acts as a defense mechanism against these changes.

Populism, although not always easy to specifically define, is generally considered a movement that accentuates the virtues and purity of a group of common people against some other: dangerous outsiders or elites who want to do harm to these common people or take away their rights or property. Thus, overplaying nationalism is a normal part of the populist toolbox. The traditional sketchy definition of populism as a political movement is based on the fact that it has no end game. It is against but not for. Only in its most extreme application, Nazism, does its "for" come into shape but then in the most repugnant and horrifying manner.

In populism, "the people"—whoever they are and whatever that phrase means—are pure and are being attacked by the outsider. Donald Trump's rhetoric—whether associating Mexican immigrants with rapists and criminals, or saying the nation's news media "is the enemy of the American people," or mentioning sovereignty twenty-one times in a United Nations speech—is a classic use of populism and "the people" to ignite and energize a political base.

In a democracy, populism is an easy and lazy answer to problems. Nothing is ever the voter's fault or responsibility, they do not need to consider how to change as the world changes, all fault lies with the vilified groups of others. The complexity of reality is never part of the populist consideration. For politicians, the same considerations apply: populism makes everything much simpler to explain, it was the other (using or not using any explicit code word for the other) that took your benefits away or caused my proposal not to succeed.

Look at the issue and the problems affecting the job market as it relates to wage growth in the United States during the second decade of the twenty-first century. The causes of these problems are literally all over the economic map. Is it because of automation and AI? Is it because so many baby boomers with higher salaries are retiring and young people entering the labor market earn lower salaries, thus somewhat distorting the figures?

Is it possible that a globalized labor supply chain is holding down wages? Whether it is manufacturing in China or coders in India, technology has made it ever easier to send work abroad. Related is the fact that in 1975, laborers received 65 percent of all income in the United States. Today, that figure is below 60 percent. If the percentage had remained the same as in 1975, American workers would have gained an extra trillion dollars per year.

Because the facts of job creation are intricate and complicated, it is easy for the populist politician to blame changes in the job market on outsourcing. President Trump consistently falls back on the argument of "bad" trade having empowered countries like China. The problem with this argument is that the facts not only are more complicated but don't even hold up as a comparison against his Chinese straw horse. For example, the decline in the labor share of income is a global phenomenon, taking place not only in the United States but also in China, Japan, and all the other major Asian countries.

In traditional—and what was always assumed to be logical— trade theory, rich countries have a lot of capital and poor countries have a lot of labor. When these countries start to trade, labor's share of income should go down in the rich countries but should rise in the poor countries, which now have all this outsourcing work to do. This transfer is not happening. Labor's share of income is dropping globally. Furthermore, figures show that in the United States, labor's share of income has fallen in both tradable and nontradable sectors, and imports have not surged beyond normal patterns.

The real solution to these problems is difficult and time-consuming, and cannot be achieved by waving a magic wand or signing an executive order. As the Brookings Institute pointed out in its Hamilton Project Paper of September 2017,

> While globalization plays a role, most research finds that it is not principally responsible for the decline in labor demand experienced by low-skilled workers. Technological change that raises the relative productivity of high-skill workers is another important factor.
>
> The manufacturing sector provides an example of how techno- logical progress can affect particular groups of workers. U.S. man- ufacturing output has increased considerably since 1973—nearly doubling in 40 years—while manufacturing employment has fallen sharply. This increase in manufacturing productivity has been accompanied by a shift from low-skilled to high-skilled workers in the industry.

On paper at least, one of the easiest solutions to this problem is education. Just look at the difference in earning power between high school graduates and college graduates. College graduates with a bachelor's degree earned $59,124, on average, in 2018, while high school graduates earned $35,256. People with less than a high school diploma earned $25,636 and had the highest unemployment rate in the country at 8 percent. In addition, according to the Economic Policy Institute, non-college-graduates had a 3 percent decline in income since 2008.

As Patricia Chen wrote in the *New York Times* on this subject on September 16, 2017,

> Certainly the kinds of jobs and salaries that high school graduates used to be able to command have dived. "That's the single most important reason we're having so much trouble," said Ron Haskins, a senior fellow at the Brookings Institution. "You have to have better skills and more knowledge to make $60,000 to $80,000 a year now than in the past."
>
> The shrinking rewards of a high school education help explain not only the stress that Americans in the workforce are feeling, but also why a larger proportion of men have dropped out altogether during their prime working ages. Work doesn't pay off the way it used to.

But how easy is it to retrain the fifty-five-year-old worker, or to adapt the American education system to the problem? No matter what, there are not instant solutions. And critically, the time frame for any possible solutions to take effect openly clashes with the immediacy demanded by social media. So, for the populist politician, the answer again becomes easy: blame outsiders, China, and India for taking American jobs and consequently preventing American workers' wages from rising.

It is difficult for any democracy, especially American democracy, to react quickly to massive changes within the country. The American system of liberal democracy, based on the rule of law, the separation of powers, pluralism, and the rights of minorities, is by definition inevitably plodding. It is a system whose natural default is gradualism, always needing time for discussion, coalition building, and compromise. Unless there is either a blatantly recognizable common national emergency such as Pearl Harbor or 9/11, which instantly unites all sides, or a superb political leader such as FDR or LBJ, liberal democracy by its very nature wallows in complacency. The natural tendency for American democracy to move slowly is reinforced by the checks-and-balances system of the Constitution that limits government's power, often giving people who are threatened by change, or the vested interest that benefits from the status quo, a veto over tomorrow.

It is easy to criticize the plodding nature of liberal democracy, especially in times of cultural and economic change. But like everything else the criticism must be based on a real comparison. During the 1930s while England, the home of liberal democracy, was struggling with the Great Depression, many of its elites looked across the channel at Germany and were envious of how efficient the German economy had become under the Nazis. Of course the English elites saw only the smoke from the German factories, not the absence of the rule of law, the lack of freedom of the press, and the roundups by the ss. As Winston Churchill stated, "Democracy is the worst form of Government except for all those other forms that have been tried from time to time."

Liberal democracy, with its need to compromise, and thus its inability to respond quickly to problems, opens the door for populism, especially when people are frightened by rapid change. Populism is not new to American democracy or to any democracy. It is the bête noir, the destructive traveling companion of democracy, always willing to take the lead in times of radical change. It is a natural human response when people are fearful of change. As Immo Fritsche, a professor at the University of Leipzig in Germany whose work focuses on group identity, shows, when people feel a loss of control, they retreat to group identity. They seek a stronger connection to the group they know and experience a desire to make their group more powerful. Essentially, to regain control, they try to make things like they used to be.

Populism promises both immediate fixes and the thrill of belonging to a country or a society that is better than others. In our era of globalization, if one is frightened of or doesn't understand—or does not want to partake in—the changes that globalization is forcing on society, then even the very idea of believing that you are special can act as a defense mechanism against these changes, at least for a time.

The writers of the U.S. Constitution spent ceaseless hours discussing how to limit or prevent populism. Ron Chernow, in his biography of Alexander Hamilton, states, "Hamilton's besetting fear was that American democracy would be spoiled by demagogues who would mouth populist shibboleths to conceal their despotism." To limit populism, the authors of the Constitution purposely inserted various provisions, such as the Electoral College, a Senate chosen by state legislatures, and lifetime seats for federal judges.

Populism in the United States as a major political force can be traced back to Andrew Jackson's election to the presidency in 1828. It then reemerged, in response to economic stress of the industrial revolution, with Williams Jennings Bryan's campaign for the presidency and his Cross of Gold speech. And during the Great Depression it was revived again by Huey Long and Father Coughlin. What is radically different in the 2016 version of American populism is that it did not begin with leftists attacking millionaires as enemies of the people. Ironically, Bryan, Long, or Coughlin would have seen Trump as the living embodiment of the high-living moneyed person, the defining enemy of the common man. All three of these men campaigned against the millionaires, the Rockefellers and their like, who in their opinion were "exploiting" the honest working people.

Huey Long, in his famous 1934 Share Our Wealth speech, epitomized this tradition when he stated "what the wise men of all ages and all times" have said: "That you must keep the wealth of the country scattered, and you must limit the amount that any one man can own. You cannot let any man own $300,000,000,000 or $400,000,000,000. If you do, one man can own all of the wealth that the United States has in it."

And at a rally in the same year, Long stated:

How many men ever went to a barbecue and would let one man take off the table what's intended for 9/10th of the people to eat? The only way to be able to feed the balance of the people is to make that man come back and bring back some of that grub that he ain't got no business with!

Now we got a barbecue. We have been praying to the Almighty to send us to a feast. We have knelt on our knees morning and nighttime. The Lord has answered the prayer. He has called the barbecue. "Come to my feast," He said to 125 million American people. But Morgan and Rockefeller and Mellon and Baruch have walked up and took 85 percent of the victuals off the table!

Now, how are you going to feed the balance of the people? What's Morgan and Baruch and Rockefeller and Mellon going to do with all that grub? They can't eat it, they can't wear the clothes, they can't live in the houses.

We've got to call Mr Morgan and Mr Mellon and Mr Rockefeller back and say, come back here, put that stuff back on this table here that you took away from here that you don't need. Leave something else for the American people to consume. And that's the program.

Historically, populism in America was not about bringing back yesterday but making tomorrow better for the common man. It had that American feel of optimism. Right-based populism is a European tradition. Interestingly, the populist closest to the American tradition in the 2016 presidential election was Bernie Sanders, with his attacks on Hillary Clinton's relationship with bankers Goldman Sachs and his call for universal free college education.

In what could easily be called the globalization of ideas, Trump's antiglobalist and populist rhetoric was practically copied word for word from the European right, a movement that sees nationalism—not sharing of wealth—as its key component. The idea of making it like it used to be, bringing back yesterday, is much more a main component of European right-wing populism than the traditional American version. Huey Long's speech, in which he talks about a chicken in every pot and every man a king, is not about bringing back yesterday but about making tomorrow into the everyman's cornucopia.

As Ronald F. Inglehart, of the University of Michigan, and Pippa Norris, of Harvard's Kennedy School, wrote in an August 2016 working paper for the Kennedy School about the populism that has overtaken Europe:

Cultural values, combined with several social and demographic factors, provide the most consistent and parsimonious explanation for voting support for populist parties; their contemporary popularity in Europe is largely due to ideological appeals to traditional values which are concentrated among the older generation, men, the religious, ethnic majorities, and less educated sectors of society. We believe that these are the groups most likely to feel that they have become strangers from the predominant values in their own country, left behind by progressive tides of cultural change which they do not share. Older white men with traditional values—who formed the cultural majority in Western societies during the 1950s and 1960s—have seen their predominance and privilege eroded. The silent revolution of the 1970s appears to have spawned an angry and resentful counter-revolutionary backlash today. In the longer-term, the generation gap is expected to fade over time, as older cohorts with traditional attitudes are gradually replaced in the population by their children and grandchildren, adhering to more progressive values. In the short-term, however, the heated culture wars dividing young and old have the capacity to heighten generational conflict, to challenge the legitimacy of liberal democracy, and to disrupt long-established patterns of party competition.

Trump's non-American approach to antiglobalization directly resonated with the European populist and nationalist right. Just take a look at the various statements from the leaders of the European populist hard right immediately after Trump won the presidential election in 2016:

Marine Le Pen, the head of France's National Front:

Donald Trump has made possible what was presented as completely impossible. So it's a sign of hope for those who cannot bear wild globalization, who cannot bear the political life led by the elites.

Frauke Petry, the leader of the party Alternative for Germany:

The election of Donald Trump is a triumph of the American people, a victory of ordinary people over the political establishment. It's a victory over the politically correct globalist elites who show little interest in the well-being of the people.

Geert Wilders, head of the Freedom Party of the Netherlands:

America regained its national sovereignty, its identity. It reclaimed its own democracy, that's why I called it a revolution. And I think that the people of America, as in Europe, feel insulted by all the politicians that ignore the real problems.

Nigel Farage, former head of the UK Independence Party in England, who even campaigned for Trump in the United States:

Brexit was the first brick that was knocked out of the establishment wall. A lot more were knocked out last night. This is Brexit times three. It is a bigger country, it is a bigger position, it is a bigger event.

The final reason that the antiglobalists will fail leads directly back to the old political adage "You can't beat someone with no one." The antiglobalist, European form of populism offers not solutions but only angry and misleading rhetoric about preventing change. The questions and the political unease that bought about populism are real. As an example, how do you tell the traditional German or Austrian citizen that immigrants are vital for their aging economy when their population rate is barely replacing itself? How do you tell the middle-aged factory worker in the United States that one of the reasons the U.S. economy is so dynamic today compared with its counterparts in Europe and Japan is that the United States has a younger population because of immigration?

And how do you tell the middle-aged factory worker in Toledo, Ohio, that his or her world is better, more peaceful, because millions are no longer dying of starvation in China? Or that manufacturing in the United States is actually increasing, with manufacturing output in the first quarter of 2017 more than 80 percent above its level thirty years ago after adjusting for inflation, when what that person sees is overall employment in manufacturing dropping daily? The individual in Toledo is not wrong in what he or she sees; manufacturing as a percentage of the national economy accounted for about 23 percent of gross output in 1997, the first year for which such data is available, but just 11.6 percent in 2018. And a third of the United States' jobs in 1953 were in manufacturing, while by 2017 that proportion had fallen to 8.5 percent. But the problem with the Toledo vision is that it is an incomplete view that does not see the full reality of the change, including its positive aspects. It is like the buggy whip factory employee railing against the advent of buses.

Populism in the European style is simple; it is great at reinforcing what people see even if what they see is an illusion, a world that never truly existed. Populists and the antiglobalists never deal with the whole picture; they never ask the second question. Instead they assume the reality they see is the full picture. They totally ignore the philosopher Rene Descartes' famous example of a simple illusion—how a pencil looks bent or misshapen when it is submerged in a bowl of water—which has been part of human knowledge since the seventeenth century. And in not fully seeing, the antiglobalists have no logical plan to improve; their only position is to remake yesterday. Trump's campaign theme, Make America Great Again, defines this position with its emphasis on *again*.

Realistically, there is no way to bring the past back. Take, for example, Trump's campaign rhetoric against various U.S. trade pacts. In reality, pulling out the current trade pacts only reroutes production and trade to other countries not in the agreements or increase automation here in the United States. And Trump's constant cry against China weakening its currency goes against the fact China is working to raise the value of its currency. The rhetoric can appear compelling, especially all the speeches on protectionism, but the truth is very different. As Michael R. Strain, the John G. Searle Scholar and director of economic policy studies at the American Enterprise Institute, wrote somewhat sarcastically in *Bloomberg* on September 26, 2017, "That taken to its logical conclusion, protectionism would find me growing all my food, sewing all my clothes, treating my own illnesses, and building my own house—all while immiserating the nation? Supporting economic silliness is fine if it helps the populists keep what they've got."

Without a doubt, globalization has been disruptive, and as in all periods of change, people who did not or could not adapt have suffered. But the answer to that suffering is not empty plans that try to lock out the world and stop the future. History is replete with countries that have closed themselves off from tomorrow, that have tried to protect their citizens from change, and in the process have not only lost power and prestige but have seen their economies whither. Whether in China after the withdrawal of the great fleet in the fifteenth century, the end of Islamic Golden Age at about the same time, Mao's China, or even the United States' withdrawal into isolationism in the 1920s, shutting one's nation off from the world is not the answer, and never has been.

The next chapter looks at how the American political system failed and allowed the counterrevolution against globalization to flourish and become a potent political force. Why did it happen? Specifically, how did the American political system not see the harm globalization was causing to a significant minority of the U.S. population? Why was the political system in the United States so deaf to how America was changing? And why did it take until the election of 2016 to see that a severe political crisis had developed?

THREE

A Disturbance in the Force

The most surprising aspect about globalization's effect on American politics is that it took until the presidential election of 2016 to see that a severe crisis, what in the *Star Wars* movies would be called "a disturbance in the force," had occurred. After all, globalization was not a recent phenomenon: it began to affect American workers in the 1970s. In fact, by 2016, in terms of job losses, outsourcing was yesterday's issue. By 2016 manufacturing jobs disappeared mainly because of automation and technology.

To act on something, however, one needs to see it and recognize it. And the failure of the American government to see that its own economic heartland and urban centers were being savaged by globalization is probably the most profound blind spot in American politics since Reconstruction. Simply put, the radical counterrevolution against globalism did not have to happen. It happened because the American democratic system failed first to see and then to harness globalization so that it would benefit the country as a whole.

One of the few American politicians who saw early on that the American industrial middle class was being thrown into chaos by globalization was Pat Buchanan, the man who helped coin the phrase "silent majority" during Richard Nixon's administration. In the mid-1990s, when he was campaigning for the presidential nomination in the Republican primaries, Buchanan spoke of how the deindustrialization of America was creating a new group of angry voters, a group not so dissimilar to his earlier "silent majority." The main difference, however, was that for these new populists—unlike Nixon's silent majority—economics trumped social issues and big business was as bad as big government.

Time magazine captured this in a piece about Pat Buchanan's 1996 Republican primary campaign, published in their February 26, 1996, edition.

"Executioners" is what he [Pat Buchanan] calls employers like AT&T that lay off thousands of workers. "These companies are like creatures in Jurassic Park," he told *Time* last week. And what will his campaign do? "Stand up for the working men and women whose jobs are threatened by unfair trade deals done for the benefit of huge corporations," he told a cheering crowd in Manchester, New Hampshire.

With great success, Republicans have been playing for decades on one enduring strand of populism, a resentment of Big Government. Buchanan has revived another that his party cannot so easily accommodate: hostility to Big Business.

Buchanan has pinpointed and energized a constituency that the G.O.P. can ill afford to lose, the Downwardly Mobile Middle Class. But he's done it with a message that the party of freewheeling capitalism can't embrace. The same righteous belligerence he turns against affirmative action, abortion and other targets of his culture war, he's now pointing at the Fortune 500.

For years the Republican solution for the grievances of the middle class have been lower taxes, less government.

What Buchanan has discovered is the enduring power of the full populist litany: moral conservatism, rejection of political elites, fear of foreigners and—the one leg that Republicans have largely avoided—suspicion of concentrated economic power.

Blue-collar voters, most of them white and male, have been crucial to the G.O.P. coalition since the late 1960s, when they started to abandon the Democrats because of everything called liberalism—meaning, roughly, racial integration plus sex, drugs and rock 'n' roll. So long as the economic grievances of those voters were secondary to their distaste for the '60s and its aftermath, the G.O.P. could court them without compromising its pro-business orthodoxies.

Now it's not so easy.

In reality, however, by the time of Buchanan's campaign for the presidency in the mid-1990s, the takeover of America's economy by globalization was all but complete. It was just being hidden behind the information technology boom of the period. American manufacturing industries had either closed or become comfortable with both outsourcing and marketing globally, while major foreign firms—particularly in the automobile industry—had established assembly plants in the United States.

Ironically, in the category "be careful of what you wish for," one of the few government plans at that time to help workers affected by globalization would later pave the way for the Great Recession. Members of the Clinton administration realized that because of global competition, it would be difficult for the wages of blue-collar workers to rise. As a result, they experimented with making it easier for these people to purchase homes. The idea was based on the belief that over time, in general, home prices consistently rise. Therefore, the net worth of homeowners would increase even though their salaries had not risen. This situation would then create what economists called the "wealth effect," an outcome based on mixing the study of human behavior with economics that implies when peoples' assets rise, they feel more secure about their wealth and will spend more.

In 1995, President Clinton wrote about expanding home ownership: "This past year, I directed HUD Secretary Henry G. Cisneros . . . to develop a plan to boost homeownership in America to an all time high by the end of this century. . . . Expanding homeownership will strengthen our nation's families and communities, strengthen our economy, and expand this country's great middle class. Rekindling the dream of homeownership for America's working families can prepare our nation to embrace the rich possibilities of the twenty-first century."

Clinton went on: "For many potential homebuyers, the lack of cash available to accumulate the required down payment and closing costs is the major impediment to purchasing a home. Other households do not have sufficient available income to make the monthly payments on mortgages financed at market interest rates for standard loan terms. Financing strategies, fueled by the creativity and resources of the private and public sectors[,] should address both of these financial barriers to homeownership."

Of course, we now know what happened when the private market followed Clinton's advice to find "creative" strategies for mortgages.

When President George W. Bush came into office, he doubled down on Clinton's experiment.

As Bush stated, "If you own something, you have a vital stake in the future of our country. The more ownership there is in America, the more vitality there is in America, and the more people have a vital stake in the future of this country."

In a 2002 speech to HUD, Bush said: "But I believe owning something is a part of the American Dream, as well. I believe when somebody owns their own home, they're realizing the American Dream. . . . And we saw that yesterday in Atlanta, when we went to the new homes of the new homeowners. And I saw with pride firsthand, the man say, welcome to my home. He didn't say, welcome to government's home; he didn't say, welcome to my neighbor's home; he said, welcome to my home. And I want that pride to extend all throughout our country."

Raghuran Rajan, the Katherine Dusak Miller Distinguished Service Professor of Finance at Booth School of Business of the University of Chicago, explains in his book *Fault Lines: How Hidden Fractures Still Threaten the World Economy*:

> Recall also that the Federal Housing Administration guaranteed mortgages. It typically focused on riskier mortgages that the agencies were reluctant to touch. Here was a vehicle that was directly under political control, and it was fully utilized. In 2000, the Clinton administration dramatically cut the minimum down payment required for a borrower to qualify for an FHA guarantee to 3 percent, increased the maximum size of mortgage it would guarantee, and halved the premiums it charged

borrowers for the guarantee. All these actions set the stage for a boom in low-income housing construction and lending.

As more money from the government-sponsored agencies flooded into financing or supporting low-income housing, the private sector joined the party. After all, they could do the math, and they understood that the political compulsions behind government actions would not disappear quickly. With agency support, subprime mortgages would be liquid, and low-cost housing would increase in price. Low risk and high return—what more could the private sector desire? Unfortunately, the private sector, aided and abetted by agency money, converted the good intentions behind the affordable-housing mandate and the push to an ownership society into a financial disaster.

Both Clinton and Bush were truly acting in an altruistic manner in trying to raise the net worth of blue-collar workers as globalization was either putting a cap on these workers' salaries or outsourcing their jobs altogether. But they were doing it on the cheap without needing to spend any political capital. It was much easier to pressure a federal agency and cajole private industry than to get legislation through Congress to create realistic programs to protect the workers hurt by globalization.

An easy way to see the changes caused by globalization's Sherman-like march through the American heartland is to compare what happened in Greenwich, Connecticut, with of all places, Northeast Philadelphia, Pennsylvania, during the 2008 presidential election. In business school, one is taught that a brand represents a promise to the consumer, what the product stands for, whether that is fashion, reliability, price, or something else. If a municipality could be a brand, then Greenwich, Connecticut—the home of forty-first president George H. W. Bush—would be the Coca-Cola of the old-line Republican Party big-business interests. With a median household income of $168,000 in 2008 among its was sixty thousand people—an income figure that takes into account police, teachers, and other service personnel—and with fifty-three spec homes at that time being offered for over $5 million each, Greenwich represents both the promise and the myth of the Republican big-business brand.

Yet on November 8, 2008, that brand failed. What shouldn't have been, was. Barack Obama won Greenwich with 53.8 percent of the vote, almost a whole point better than his national average of 52.9 percent.

At the same time, Obama's 2008 share of the vote in Northeast Philadelphia's Ward 63, was only 51.67 percent. Like the Republican symbol of the elephant in Greenwich, the political brand of the donkey was represented by Northeast Philly; the Democrats had dominated the landscape of Northeast Philly since the New Deal. But in 2008 the donkey no longer appeared to fulfill its promise.

For the four previous presidential elections, the Democrats had carried Ward 63 in Northeast Philadelphia by an average margin of 13.25 percent; in 2008 it was under 5 percent. For sure, some of the erosion from the Democratic Party in Ward 63 could be attributed to the newness of an African American running for president, but as in Greenwich, something else was going on in Northeast Philadelphia.

The streets of Ward 63 have not changed much in their appearance since the Great Depression. They resemble any blue-collar neighborhood of nicely kept row houses in the United States. Walking through neighborhoods in Queens or Yonkers, New York, or Cleveland or Akron, Ohio—if not for the difference in cars' license plates—one could easily believe they were in Northeast Philadelphia.

Unlike Greenwich, Connecticut, however, Northeast Philadelphia over the past thirty years has changed in the occupational description of its residents. Northeast Philadelphia, like other old American manufacturing centers, was the battlefield where America's traditional manufacturing industries lost the war against globalization.

The residents of Greenwich can still be described as corporate leaders, financiers, private investors of various sorts, and now tech entrepreneurs. In general—except for the tech part—these same descriptions have been in place since Greenwich became a premier suburb of New York City in the early part of the twentieth century. In sharp contrast, residents of Northeast Philadelphia can no longer lay claim to the title of textile workers, shipbuilders, or steamfitters.

The residents of Greenwich have skill sets and assets that globalization demands: essentially capital, the knowledge of how to apply and use that capital, and trained entrepreneurial skills. Like residents of other more affluent urban and suburban areas in America, many Greenwich residents are now members of the newocracy, America's new aristocracy, people who are the real beneficiaries of globalization: the multinational manager, the technologist, and the aspirational members of the meritocracy. The residents of Northeast Philadelphia are not quite as lucky.

Philadelphia, especially Northeast Philadelphia, was once an economic powerhouse. For years the "Made in Philadelphia" label was as ubiquitous as today's "Made in China": "Made in Philadelphia" appeared on Baldwin locomotives, Bromley carpets, Disston saws, Cramp ships and submarines, Fitler cordage, Fels soap, Curtis magazines, Budd car and rail bodies, Horstmann silk and swords, Schoenhut toys, Reach baseballs, Gillinder glassware, Belber luggage, Meyer pianos, Yellin ironwork, Morse elevators, Remmey bricks, Wetherill paints, Johnson printing type, Flexible Flyer sleds, Warren-Knight survey instruments, White dental tools, Wilde yarn, Atlantic Refining oils, and thousands of other products.

Even as late as 1980, a significant portion of Northeast Philadelphia's workforce was still employed in shipbuilding; today, the number is insignificant. The massive local textile industry began to dissipate in the 1960s and 1970s, leaving little of manufacturing capacity by 1980.

Today major employment in Northeast Philadelphia is concentrated not in a handful of large factories but in a myriad of retail shops and small business, as well as local government service positions. Yet it was not only in Northeast Philadelphia where traditional blue-collar occupations were dying; it was throughout the country. In 1978 the most common jobs in the country were secretaries, machine operators, and factory workers. By 2014 the most common job in over thirty states was being a truck driver, a distributor—not a maker—of goods.

Northeast Philadelphia, like the other older manufacturing areas throughout the United States, had become a modern-day version of the battle of Agincourt. In that early Renaissance battle, King Charles VI of France—suffering from malaise and having his knights weighed down with technologically outdated suits of heavy armor—failed to appreciate that warfare had changed with the English introduction of the longbow. Now, like King Charles of France, it was the American political system that suffered from malaise, not realizing that the world had changed.

It wasn't just Congress that was blind; it was also the party leaders and the president. Obviously, the Obama political machine in 2008 had to be aware that although they made tremendous inroads into newocracy-rich Greenwich, Connecticut, their strength in Northeast Philly—the traditional blue-collar, Franklin Roosevelt voters—declined significantly. Didn't anyone ever question why? Didn't anyone in the campaign and then in the Obama administration realize that switching party alignment in the United States is personally not easy? Quite the opposite; it is uprooting family and historic tradition.

It is possible that Obama's myopic view was based in part on intellectual arrogance and reverse prejudice. After all, in the Democratic primary six months before, he lost many blue-collar voters to Hillary Clinton. His campaign also believed that his new coalition—made up of nonwhite Americans, younger voters, and members of the newocracy—could win without having to deal with the refugees from globalization. There was also probably a sense that the "unions" could still deliver voters en masse. In reality, the fear caused by the economic crash of 2008 probably kept enough old-line Roosevelt voters in the Democratic Party for Obama to still pull out a small win in the district. Eight years later, this did not happen when Hillary Clinton ran against Donald Trump.

Brilliantly analyzing the situation at the end of Obama's term and shortly after Trump's victory, Eduardo Porter wrote in the *New York Times* on December 18, 2016:

Did the white working class vote its economic interests?

Yes, the economy has added millions of jobs since President Obama took office. Still, less-educated white voters had a solid economic rationale for voting against the status quo—nearly all the gains from the economic recovery have passed them by.

Despite accounting for less than 15 percent of the labor force, Hispanics got more than half of the net additional jobs. Blacks and Asians also gained millions more jobs than they lost. But whites, who account for 78 percent of the labor force, lost more than 700,000 net jobs over the nine years.

This lopsided racial sorting of jobs is only one of the fault lines brought to the fore by the presidential election.

Only 472 counties voted for Hillary Clinton on Election Day. But, they account for 64 percent of the nation's *economic activity*. The 2,584 counties where Mr. Trump won, by contrast, generated only 36 percent of America's prosperity.

Non-Hispanic whites account for 62 percent of the population. But they make up some 78 percent of the population of nonmetropolitan areas and 71 percent of that of small cities, according to the demographer William H. Frey from Brookings. By contrast, they account for only 56 percent of the population of the 100 largest urban areas in the country.

Problem is, many of the jobs created since the economy started recovering from recession were in service industries, located primarily in large metropolitan areas—not in small towns and rural areas.

Even as the typical American household experienced the fastest income growth on record last year, median household income outside of metropolitan areas fell 2 percent, according to the Census Bureau.

Eduardo Porter's piece misses one horrifying social problem that was occurring at the same time; the opiate epidemic that mirrored the economic changes that were taking place. As University of California–Davis epidemiologist Magdalena Cerda stated: "The epidemic is a perfect storm. After the 2008 recession, rural areas consistently lagged behind urban areas in the recovery, losing jobs and population. You have a situation where people might be particularly vulnerable to perhaps using prescription opioids to self-medicate a lot of symptoms of distress related to sources of chronic stress, chronic economic stress."

Historically, large-scale self-medication into a less stressful state is not a new phenomenon during periods of economic upheaval and change. In Britain during the early part of the industrial revolution, when hundreds of thousands rural people migrated to the London slums for low-paying industrial work, their solace became the gin mills. It is estimated that in the mid-1700s, one-third of the buildings in London were occupied by gin shops or distilleries. Alcoholism was so rampant in London of the 1700s that even with the massive immigration into the city, the city's population declined; people drank themselves to death.

Like London in the 1700s, today's refugees from globalization are indirectly and directly committing suicide. According to the governor of Ohio's cabinet-level Opiate Action Team, there had been a 366 percent increase in drug overdose deaths from 2000 to 2012, and overdoses had become the leading cause of accidental death in Ohio. In roughly the same period, the U.S. Centers for Disease Control and Prevention reported that the suicide rate for men forty-five to sixty-four years of age had increased by 43 percent from 1999 to 2014.

Globalization's economic effect on rural America as jobs shifted from small towns to the major globalized cities went hand and hand with the opiate epidemic. For example, globalization has given New York City an amazing advantage: connecting workers in finance, service, and tech industries easily to firms and customers around the world allow New York's residents to enjoy real gains from scale and specialization. These gains in New York and other leading metropolitan areas, however, created major downsides in other areas of the country, adding fuel to the counterrevolution. First, they caused a substantial brain drain when many of the brightest young people left rural America for opportunities in the metropolitan areas. Second—and possibly more important—as wealth creation significantly migrated to the larger metropolitan areas, it created a stifling new anger against the elites in these metropolitan areas.

Using London and southern England as an example of this phenomenon and somewhat sarcastically using the French term *sans culottes*, which refers to the poor Parisian supporters of the French Revolution who could not afford underpants, the noted economist Paul Collier states in the *Times Literary Supplement* of January 25, 2017,

> So what are these people angry about? Partly their gripes are economic. The fortunes of the new elite have risen, often undeservedly, while those of the *sans cool* have deteriorated. Anger is tinged with fear: for the *sans cool* economic security is collapsing. But anger and fear go beyond the economic: people see that the members of the educated southern/coastal elite are intermarrying ("assortative mating") and embracing a globalized identity, while asserting their moral superiority by encouraging their favoured priority groups to elevate characteristics such as ethnicity and sexual orientation into exclusive "community" identities. The *sans cool* understand that both the withdrawal by the elite and the emergence of new favoured groups apparently creaming off benefits weaken their claim to help, just as their need for support is increasing. Effectively—and pragmatically—addressing these three concerns of the *sans cool* is the challenge facing our leaders.

So again: Where was the government? How was it possible that these problems were ignored and allowed to fester until they exploded into the now Trump-led counterrevolution? In retrospect, what is so surprising about the lack of the American government's response to the downsides of globalization was that it broke with historic precedent. During previous periods of severe economic disruption, the American government expanded its powers to adjust to situations that could never have been foreseen in 1788, when the Constitution was written. In the latter part of nineteenth century and the early part of the twentieth, as it became apparent that America's industrial revolution was mutating from an engine of spectacular economic growth into a monopolistic vehicle threatening America's basic democratic principles, the Progressive movement in the name of Theodore Roosevelt, William Howard Taft, and Woodrow

Wilson expanded the role of government to corral the forces created by the industrial revolution. Broad changes such as the Interstate Commerce Commission, the Federal Trade Commission, the Food and Drug Administration, the IRS, and the Federal Reserve were introduced both to limit the power of monopolies and to try to correct the abuses of the Gilded Age.

Like the populist movement that supported Trump and Sanders in the 2016 election, a populist movement had grown up in the United States late in the nineteenth century to fight the inequities caused by the industrial revolution. The U.S. presidential elections of 1896 and 1900—both won by William McKinley, with Theodore Roosevelt as McKinley's vice presidential running mate in the 1900 election—were fought over issues analogous to those of the 2016 election, with some important differences. The 1896 election in particular could almost be called the "city versus country" election. Simply put, it pitted the economic interests of the booming new industrialized cities and new technologies against the populist rural interests championed by William Jennings Bryan. The major difference between the 2016 election and the elections during the industrial revolution, however, was that the counterrevolutionist populists lost to the new industries in both 1896 and 1900. Another difference—which occurred mainly after McKinley was assassinated and Roosevelt assumed the presidency—was that many of Bryan's issues were absorbed into the progressive platform and became law, including the graduated income tax, direct election of senators, initiative, referendum, recall, and the secret ballot.

Thirty-two years later, in response to the Great Depression, the powers of the federal government were again expanded exponentially, creating agencies and commissions such as Social Security, the Tennessee Valley Authority, and the Security and Exchange Commission, all of which could never have been imagined by America's Founding Fathers. The Franklin Roosevelt administration not only created a safety net for the industrial worker but also saved and preserved America's liberal capitalist system from the lure of fascism or communism.

Similar to these previous periods of economic change in the

United States, globalization has destroyed the perception of equilibrium in American society. It has created a divide within the democracy, between those whose career prospects appear unlimited, and the factory workers and service industries employees who cater to them and whose career prospects are eroding.

So why wasn't there any major government action to help the people who had become the refugees of globalization, people whose job skills could not gain them entrance into the newocracy?

Former Speaker of the House Tip O'Neill was fond of saying that "all politics is local," and normally this motto is ironclad. Who has their feet and ears on the ground more often than members of the House of Representatives, who must have their employment contract with the public renewed every two years? So again why weren't there any political action? Why wasn't there an uproar in Congress? The answer is possibly gerrymandering—which severely hinders political competitiveness—but more likely it is that the governing philosophy of the United States had radically shifted. The American political system failed to provide a safety net to those whose economic lives were upended by globalization because frankly it tuned these people out.

The United States was born with two opposing philosophies of government. The first, promulgated by Alexander Hamilton, called for a strong national government supporting economic growth. The other, supported by Thomas Jefferson, called for limited government, especially for the federal government. In 1980, with the election of Ronald Reagan and the Republican Party, the American government became officially Jeffersonian.

Reagan created a political environment that not only rejected government intervention but saw it as harmful to America's democracy. This view was celebrated with slogans such as "the government that governs best governs least" and Reagan's well-known quip "the most terrifying words in the English language are: 'I'm from the government and I'm here to help.'"

The post–World War II and Cold War Republican Party before Reagan had been a party of economic conservatism but not necessarily the party of limited government. For example, under the Eisenhower administration, the interstate highway system was created, while under the Nixon administration the Environmental Protection Agency was formed and the Clean Air Act was passed. Furthermore, Nixon championed the idea of revenue sharing, where the federal government would be the aggregator of funds and then would pass those funds to the states, believing that local jurisdictions could solve the problems more efficiently and with less red tape. Revenue sharing did not mean that government had no function in solving problems; rather, it was a vehicle in the Nixon administration view to rebalance federalism. The State and Local Assistance Act of 1972, the official name for Nixon's revenue sharing, had distributed to the states over $83 billion before President Reagan eliminated it in 1986.

The Reagan administration saw the role of government and its relationship to the individual very differently from Eisenhower and Nixon. As the Heritage Foundation reported on January 20, 1981, in commenting on Ronald Reagan's first inaugural address: "Reagan presents himself as a follower of the Constitution. 'Our Government,' he emphasizes, 'has no power except that granted it by the people. It is time to check and reverse the growth of government which shows signs of having grown beyond the consent of the governed.' The old Constitution, with its restraints and emphasis on limited government, allows individual freedom to work for the common good. 'In this present crisis, government is not the solution to our problem; government is the problem.'"

But there are two major problems with this view, notwithstanding the fact it still resonates within the current congressional wing of the Republican Party now, decades since Reagan was first inaugurated. First, amazingly it fails to recognize that the Constitution was an operating document written for the problems of a 1789 world. Second, it fails to appreciate collective worldwide forces such as globalization that are more powerful than most individuals' abilities to respond. And if these forces are left unchecked they can damage the very balance that makes up our democracy.

In addition to establishing the philosophical construct that limited government is a more important value than protecting Americans from the harshness of a rapidly changing economy, the Reagan revolution substantially expanded the traditional Republican base by attracting the so-called Reagan Democrats. These new Republicans were—and are—white working-class voters, primarily from the Midwest and the Northeast, who deserted what they saw as a Democratic Party that had grown too liberal. They believed that the Democratic Party was trying to correct age-old social problems at their expense. The Reagan Democrats, following on the inroads that Nixon had made with the silent majority, would spearhead a blue-collar movement of middle- and working-class white people—especially men—into the GOP.

Donald Trump's appeal to these people—those most left behind by the changes in the American economy—defined both the major contradiction and failure of Reaganism. As long as the Reagan Democrats' prime concerns were social, it was easy for the Republican Party to, if not directly respond to their needs, at least keep these people placated. Once the needs of these voters were economically based and required government action, however, the path that would have enabled such action had been prevented by the very Jeffersonian revolution these people had joined.

It was not only the Republican Party, however, that was blind to the negative impacts of globalization; the Democrats, ironically partly because of globalization, had lost their union soul. During Franklin Roosevelt's New Deal in the 1930s, if the president wanted to know how policy would affect blue-collar workers, it is reported that he typically said to an aide, "Call Sydney." FDR was referring to Sydney Hillman, the head of the Amalgamated Clothing Workers of America and the first chairperson of the Congress of Industrial Organizations' political action committee. But by the late 1980s there was no Sydney to call. The U.S. clothing industry had moved most of its manufacturing to Asia. And naturally as blue-collar manufacturing jobs left the United States, union membership rapidly declined.

Elections are won in the United States because of the ability of the parties to organize voter turnout, what is commonly known in politics as GOTV (get out the vote). As union membership diminished, the ability of unions to deliver bloc votes to Democratic candidates also diminished. To win elections the Democratic Party had to expand and refocus its issues to meet the needs of its new base, primarily nonwhite Americans, younger voters, and members of the newocracy. Blue-collar workers who had been a major force within the Democratic Party before globalization had become a minority within the party's coalition. And in this process the Democratic Party lost the ability to hear the needs of the refugees of globalization, and these refugees lost the organizational clout that they previously had to influence the party.

As the descendants of Pat Buchanan rank and file have seized control of the Republican coalition, former Republican political buzzwords have changed in their meaning. For the new populist Republicans, championing free enterprise and individual rights means something very different from the traditional Republican approach of championing big business, a tradition that had gone back to the Hamiltonian philosophy and Lincoln's Whig roots, with government support of canals and railroad rights of way. For these new noncorporate members of the Republican Party, government support of big business—whether through regulations, the 2008 Troubled Asset Relief program, bailouts, or investments in solar energy—is anathema.

These new Republicans would also be those most negatively affected by globalization and what they saw as globalization's traveling companion, immigration.

Where the newocracy sees globalization as the future and something to profit from, the new Republican populists for good reason see it as a direct threat to their income and way of life. There is no more important issue that defines this split than immigration. As Fareed Zakaria wrote in a brilliant piece on populism in the November-December 2016 issue of *Foreign Affairs*: "Immigration is the final frontier of globalization. It is the most intrusive and disruptive because as a result of it, people are dealing not with objects or abstractions; instead, they come face-to-face with other human beings, ones who look, sound, and feel different."

Although many of these new Republicans were grandchildren and great-grandchildren of immigrants, they perceive immigration into the United States as a major threat. For those who have been left behind by globalization, immigration represents much that is wrong with the world today. To these people, there is little difference between American jobs going overseas and, because of open borders or simplified visa requirements, immigrants coming into the United States. Either way, they feel, foreigners, that is, globalization, have taken opportunities away from them.

In hindsight, of course the counterrevolution against globalization within the United States was not difficult to forecast. For decades, the issues that it coalesced around festered: massive trade-related economic dislocation, some regions of the nation benefiting far more than others, the Democrats ignoring what used to be their base while the Republicans played their new base for their votes while ignoring their economic interests. Added to these factors are two other components we will be discuss in the next two chapters: America's misunderstanding of what constitutes global leadership as globalization began to emerge and, of course, the advent of the human capital economy, technology, and social media.

FOUR

How *Downton Abbey* Resonates in America Today

From 2010 to 2015, people in the United States were mesmerized by the British television series *Downton Abbey*. Then in 2019 a major movie was based on the TV series. The series and the movie were a fictional account of the trials and tribulations of an aristocratic English family named the Crawleys, who were living on a magnificent, inherited Georgian-era estate. The fictionalized story detailed how the family had to adapt to change between 1912 and 1926, as it became increasingly difficult to keep up the aristocratic, servant-laden British country lifestyle.

Even in 1912, the year the series' plot began, that lifestyle was already a mirage, no longer in any realistic way economically sustainable. In fact, the family in the story was able to keep up the pretense of their lifestyle only because the patriarch of the family had married an American millionairess whose father was a supposed founder of a large American department store. Interestingly, this fictionalized marriage—for both love and the refilling of the family's bank account—was not so dissimilar to many real-life British aristocrats at that time. In fact, Lord Randolph Churchill—Winston Churchill's father—married Jenny Jerome, the daughter of an American financier and real-estate speculator.

If there was a hypothetical prequel to *Downton Abbey*, it probably would begin in 1846, when the British landowning families were hit by an economic tsunami forcing them into economic decline over the following decades. That tsunami was triggered by a change in the British tariff system, which we know as the repeal of the Corn Laws.

In proper British English, "corn" is more than just the yellow grain we eat on the cob in the United States. The word *corn* in England refers to any multitude of cereal grains, whether it is wheat from Britain or oats from Ireland. The Corn Laws were high tariffs on importing these grains, which were being grown at that time far less expensively in the United States, Canada, and South America.

The political logic of the high duties on grain was indisputable. The noninherited revenue stream of the landowning British aristocracy, who controlled many of the votes in Parliament through a system called rotten boroughs, was based partly on the growing of grain in England. The high tariffs halted food imports and made the large estates hugely profitable. The tariffs basically gave the so-called landed gentry a monopoly over British food production.

After a twenty-six-year struggle in Parliament culminating in 1846, the Corn Laws were repealed for two primary reasons. First, it was the heyday of the industrial revolution in England. As British prime minister Benjamin Disraeli stated a couple of years after the repeal, England had become "the workshop of the world," in many ways analogous to the United States and the modern tech industry. The new British manufacturers wanted free trade; they did not want other countries putting up barriers to their products to counter the English trade barriers. Along with this repeal went David Ricardo's theory of comparative advantages, which had recently come into political vogue. Ricardo's theory, as we discussed in chapter 1, was that a country should concentrate its resources on what it produces most efficiently, and for England in the nineteenth century that was steam engines, steel, and textiles, which most other countries lacked the ability to produce. Consequently, a focus on agriculture diverted resources away from Britain's uniquely well-developed manufacturing capabilities.

The other reason the Corn Laws were repealed was the fear that the continuation would lead to food riots in the growing industrial cities. As people moved off the land into factories in massive numbers, it was important for the stability of the society that food be inexpensive and affordable for these people.

The repeal of the Corn Laws—albeit after two and a half decades of political struggle—was the beginning of the end of the economic viability of the landed aristocratic elites of Britain. It was also a clear demonstration that for an economy to move forward, a government cannot favor the old elites, old industries, and old ways of doing business to the detriment of the new.

A majority vote in Parliament to repeal the Corn Laws, however, could not have happened before a more important reform, the 1832 Reform Act, occurred. The Reform Act was essentially the recognition by Parliament of the massive changes the growing industrial revolution was having on English society. The act placated the increasing unrest of the new industrial-based middle class through expanding the franchise—the right to vote—to residents of the newly industrialized cities. It granted representation in Parliament to the large new industrial cities such as Birmingham and Manchester and removed seats from what were known as the aforementioned "rotten boroughs." These rotten boroughs were areas where few people still lived but had representatives in Parliament. They were controlled primarily by the large agricultural estates. For example, the borough of Old Sarum at Salisbury had two members of Parliament but only seven voters. In addition to rotten boroughs, there was also what was known as "pocket" boroughs, owned by major landowners who chose their own members of Parliament.

As reforms go, the Reform Act of 1832 was middling at best. It is always difficult to get vested interests to vote against their own immediate interest for the sake of the country. The act, among other things, increased the electorate from about five hundred thousand to eight hundred thousand, making about one in five adult males eligible to vote for parliamentary representatives. However, it had little real impact on the lives of the working classes and failed to introduce a secret ballot. What it did, though, was significantly reduce the power of the landed gentry, the vested interests who benefited from government support of the old agriculture-based economy.

So how does the fictional financial deterioration of the Crawley family and the twenty-six-year struggle to repeal the Corn Laws in England relate to the United States in the first quarter of the twenty-first century? Simply put, the current situation in America is a similar fight between the old ways of doing business and the new for government support. Like the aristocratic estates in England in the 1840s, the old industries in the United States no longer offer the country a comparative advantage, but on account of the power of vested interest they still have a significant voice within the government.

The 2016 election in America in fact was much more than just a fight about how disgruntled workers in Michigan, Indiana, or Pennsylvania were supposedly hurt by globalization. It was a battle for government support between America's old industries, whose roots go back to the industrial revolution, and America's new globalized industries: coal versus clean energy, steel versus Apple, domestic oil against electric cars, yesterday versus the globalized companies of tomorrow.

Historically, of course, there are always such fights. What made 2016 particularly different is the change in industries was not a gradual progression, like movies to TV. Instead, it was a radical change in the industrial and, thus, cultural environment. In fact it was similar to but even faster than what the Crawley family went through during the industrial revolution in England, when the British economy changed from agrarian and craft-based to heavy manufacturing.

There are two major economic and political differences, however, between the Crawleys' Britain and the United States today. First, the fight in the United States is not about government support to protect the income flow of the landed gentry but about protecting investors and the workers in the declining asset-based industries such as steel and coal over the new globalized tech-based industries.

Second, the United States has a written constitution—a point that will be discussed further in the final chapter. Although there was a major political struggle to pass the Reform Act, because England does not have a written constitution, parliament had the power to change its representation process without going through a complicated procedure like the one set forth in the U.S. Constitution. The English parliament of 1832 had the flexibility to rapidly realign itself to reflect the new economic reality of that era. Contrast that with the U.S. Congress of today. The Constitution was written in 1787 and thus reflects the agrarian economy of that time. But consider how the 1787 operating system called the Constitution has disenfranchised tomorrow. California, with a population at this writing of approximately thirty-nine million people has two senators, while Montana, with a population of one million people, also has two senators. Obviously, yesterday's industries—ranching and farming, which are prevalent in Montana—have more say under the U.S. constitutional system than California's Silicon Valley, a situation not so dissimilar to the rotten borough system before the Reform Act.

Putting constitutional questions aside for the moment, what has made the United States able to be the principal creator of the knowledge age is its ability to adapt to change, an ability derived from the United States' cultural respect for the freedom to take risks, to innovate, and to be entrepreneurial. But innovation by definition brings about change, creating new winners and challenging the power and the cultural mores of entrenched interests that had become accustomed to the status quo. Unlike global trade, innovation and finding new ways of doing things often is a zero-sum game with winners and losers. Examples are scattered throughout the economic and business history of the United States. Just look at how the airline industry destroyed the profitability of the railroads.

How long the losers survive, and how quickly the winners can continue to grow, is partly determined by which industries get support and protection from the American government, and which do not. We are taught that in the United States, business and government are independent of each other, but in reality that is pure fiction. Just look at how many lobbyists there are in Washington, working on behalf of various industrial and commercial interests. The reality is that America likes to talk the ideas of Jeffersonian limited government that I mentioned in chapter 2, but in reality—especially in terms of supporting industry—America is Hamiltonian.

For instance, today in the United States the old-line industries want government protection from imports with penalizing duties, much as the British aristocrats wanted high duties against foreign grain. And the new industries in America today support free trade, just as the British steam engine or steel manufacturers of the nine-

85

teenth century did. While "Made in America" is an important slogan for U.S Steel, for Apple—which relies on global sourcing and the global exchange of ideas—it is a relic of the past.

Consider the industrial leaders who backed President Trump and the main donors to the Republican National Committee: they are primarily investors in the old fixed-asset economy of America, while the new leaders of American corporate life, the Silicon Valley entrepreneurs and executives, primarily backed Hillary Clinton.

Although Trump—the candidate of the old industries—won the election, it is difficult to imagine, even with the bias in the U.S. Constitution against change, that the old industries can continue to commandeer government support for a substantial period. Look at Trump's protectionist crusade against China in support of American steel at the start of his administration and ask yourself which side will eventually win. The steel industry in the United States in 2018 employed one-sixth of 1 percent of the American workforce, approximately eighty-one thousand workers, while ironically the steel-importing industry employed over sixty thousand workers in the United States. Without a doubt, the steel industry over the past twenty years has been hemorrhaging workers. Steel jobs nationally have fallen dramatically, down from 135,000 jobs in 2000. By the way, as an example of how America and the world have changed, in 1953 there were 650,000 people employed in the steel industry in the United States.

But the decline in steel employment over the last several decades has little to do with imports; the cause is primarily automation. The truth is that in the late 1970s, it took ten workers to make a ton of steel, while today it takes only one. Putting it another way, in 1980 it took 10.1 man-hours to make a ton of steel, while in 2019 it took 1.5 man-hours. Basically, Trump's steel tariffs were a placebo to working-class voters, trying to bring back a world that no longer exists, while for American steel mill management and shareholders, the tariffs at least theoretically offered the ability to raise prices and increase profitability.

On the other hand, the American auto industry is a truly globalized player, with its integrated global sourcing, manufacturing, and marketing. China is now GM's largest market, with eleven joint-venture plants that produced and delivered more than 3.8 million vehicles in 2016. Or look at Apple, whose second-largest market is in China. A trade war with China to protect the U.S. steel industry threatens GM and Apple. A trade war might make sense as political rhetoric to feed the base, but in reality it is harmful to tomorrow's economy.

Look at Boeing, in many ways the crown jewel of American sophisticated manufacturing. Although it assembles its planes in the United States, it sources the parts for these planes from all over the world. Parts for Boeing's 787 Dreamliner come from five thousand factories worldwide. The forward fuselage comes from Japan, the engines from England, the entry doors from France, and the rudder from China. The Boeing 787 might be trademarked "Made in America," but in the air it is the flying definition of globalization, a true mutt.

The 787 represents another sharp contrast between the old industries and the new. The new industries straddle globalization, seeing the world itself as the marketplace, understanding that in order to sell to the world, they need to buy from the world. Boeing would need to shrink tremendously as a company to be a supplier of just domestic commercial aircraft, as approximately 70 percent of Boeing Commercial Airplanes' revenue comes from customers outside the United States. GE is similar, as in 2017 almost 70 percent of its revenues will be from outside the United States. In order to sell to the world and not create local foreign pressure to build competing commercial aircraft factories, Boeing—like GE—recognizes that it must share the wealth by sourcing across the world.

Just look at the representatives of industry in Trump's cabinet contrasted with the people who backed Clinton. But—like the counter-revolution itself—even though the candidate of the old industries won the election, the reality is that the old industries have already lost the war. Trump's supporters will be given some short-term government goodies, whether through higher tariffs or tax support, but in the long term it will not be enough for these companies to continue to flourish and survive. Ask yourself who is more important to the U.S. economy today: Apple—which has little influence on any specific electoral votes—or the coal and steel industry, which can influence the electoral votes of Kentucky, West Virginia, and Pennsylvania? Globalization has been fully integrated into the most dominant aspects of the American economy, whether it is aerospace or agriculture, computers or finance, and all the talk about protectionism and the evils of various trade pacts won't change that.

The integration of globalization into the American economy, combined with the impact of globalized mores via social media on American consumer companies, has assured the eventual political victory of the new industries over the old. And these forces will lead to the eventual defeat of the counterrevolution against globalization. Two obvious examples stand out. First, the 2017 race for the U.S. Senate seat in Alabama between Doug Jones—the eventual winner—and Roy Moore was, among other things, a clear victory for globalization in a state where the world *globalization* is anathema. Not only did Jones back NAFTA—an economic win-win for Alabama—he constantly hammered on the fact that Moore's extremely conservative social stances would drive international automobile manufacturers away from the state.

What Roy Moore failed to realize was that globalization and the concept of the international manufacturing supply chain had successfully begun to replace the plantation culture of Alabama. As of 2016 in Alabama, Mercedes, Hyundai, Honda, and Toyota provided more than fifty-seven thousand jobs that produced 1.7 million automobile engines for both domestic use and export. Transportation equipment had become Alabama's number one export.

Another example is in North Carolina, where globalized mores won the battle over more regional and traditional views. The state legislature in March 2016 passed the so-called bathroom bill, which blocked the Obama administration's executive order for transgender bathrooms. In response to this action, major corporations and organizations that were planning investments or activities in North Carolina put their actions on hold. The Associated Press calculated that the legislature's bathroom bill would cost the state of North Carolina over $3.76 billion in business revenue. PayPal dropped plans to build a facility that would have added an estimated $2.66 billion to the state's economy, and Deutsche Bank dropped plans for 250 jobs in the Raleigh area. Adidas—which was planning to build its first U.S. sports shoe factory in High Point, North Carolina—switched its plans to Atlanta, Georgia, and the National Basketball Association decided to boycott the state, usually a favorite host for playoff games.

As Bank of America's CEO Brian Moynihan, head of the largest company in North Carolina, said to the World Affairs Council of Charlotte, North Carolina: "Companies are moving to other places because they don't face an issue that they face here. . . . What's going on that you don't know about? What convention decided to take you off the list? What location for a distribution facility took you off the list? What corporate headquarters consideration for a foreign company—there's a lot of them out there—just took you off the list because they just didn't want to be bothered with the controversy? That's what eats you up."

The actions and threats by consumer corporations not to do business in North Carolina forced the legislature to reconsider their position. On March 30, 2017—almost a year after the original bathroom law went into effect—a new law passed by the North Carolina legislature and signed by the governor rescinded most of the original bathroom bill. The forces of globalization had trounced regional cultural values. Globalization-derived international social media have become the new Greek chorus of corporate and brand status. Now where the brand stands on social values has become an intricate definition of the brand. Although the North Carolina legislature for sure represented a local constituency with local values, the size of that constituency was just not relevant against the size of the globalized consumer brand.

The corporate reaction to the bathroom law should not have been a surprise to the North Carolina legislature. The pressure put on the corporate brand by social media in defending globalized mores and standards could trace its origins back to Bangladesh, a country that in culture, religion, and economics could not be more different from North Carolina.

On November 24, 2012, a horrendous fire in the Tazreen Fashion factory, in the Ashulia district on the outskirts of Dhaka, Bangladesh, killed at least 112 garment workers and injured 200 others. The fire, thought to be caused by a short circuit, started on the ground floor of the nine-story factory, trapping the workers on the floors above. In an inquiry afterward, the fire department's operations manager, Mohammad Mahbub, stated, "The factory lacked the adequate emergency exits that would have made it possible to escape from the building, especially since the fire broke out in the warehouse on the ground floor and quickly moved up to higher floors. Structurally, the building's three staircases went to the ground floor, making it impossible to use in a fire originating on the ground floor, thus trapping the workers on the upper floors."

Sadly, horrendous fires in garment factories and sweatshops are not new. The most infamous one in the United States was the Triangle Shirtwaist Factory fire in New York City in 1911. That fire led to the death of 146 garment workers, and subsequently to serious changes in factory safety standards pushed by political reformers such as Fiorello La Guardia and the growing U.S. labor movement. Like the Triangle fire, the Bangladesh fire also forced the government to initiate reforms in reference to the safety standard. But a major difference in why these reforms were initiated in the 101 years separating the two disasters was that the fire in Bangladesh took place as technologically driven social media became linked to globalization.

Whether Bangladesh in 2011 had La Guardia–type reformers or an emerging labor movement was irrelevant. The pressure for reforms came from the global consumer. In 1911 no one would have thought to put pressure on Macy's or Sears not to buy from the Triangle factory because of the fire. But in 2011, as the news of the Bangladesh fire spread around the world, extensive pressure via social media was put on Walmart, Benetton, and other direct and indirect customers of the Tazreen factory and other factories in Bangladesh, insisting that unless conditions improve, these companies move their production out of Bangladesh. With the export of garment and textiles rapidly becoming the main driver of Bangladesh's economy, the government had no other choice but to comply and reform their safety standards.

Not so dissimilar to the election in Alabama, a globalized social media Greek chorus pressured the globalized brands—and consequently, Bangladesh itself—to enforce modern social mores or lose value. For sure, globalized mores were not the only reason that Roy Moore lost the election in Alabama, but like the pressure for reforms in Bangladesh, the informal pact between social media and globalization now represents a powerful new constituency that must be heard.

The political need to keep dying industries alive through establishing Maginot Lines of high tariffs—as well as the subsequent economic harm—happens not just in the United States but around the world, in both democracies and autocracies.

Consider China, where the legitimacy of the government has now evolved into a system based on the economic and social well-being of the people. The ancient imperial Chinese concept of the Mandate of Heaven—where if the emperor does not rule wisely he or she will lose heaven's mandate and be overthrown—has now become dependent on economic growth. In Chinese historic mythology, heaven would demonstrate its loss of confidence in the emperor by allowing the occurrence of earthquakes, famine, or other disasters. Today, heaven's lack of confidence would be demonstrated by crashing markets. The legitimacy of the Chinese Communist Party is now directly based on ever-rising living standards. The risk here is that the legitimacy of the party in power is based on the vicissitudes of markets, which is a difficult plank to walk if there ever was one.

The challenge facing the Chinese government is massive. How does one reengineer a gigantic—and relatively slowing—investment-led economy into being a more balanced consumer-driven economy, without causing some unemployment, which would threaten the legitimacy that the government is based on? The way the Chinese government has been dealing with this problem is by doing the opposite of a Maginot-like tariff solution but with similar effect. China is allowing its dated, inefficient state-owned companies, in particular those in the steel industry, to continue to operate and accumulate large debt, just to prevent unemployment in these industries.

In the interlinked globalized world, where every action has a reaction, the policy of the Chinese government to move slowly on closing inefficient plants has caused a legitimate feeding frenzy among the antiglobalists and can even be directly linked to one of antiglobalism's earliest major successes: Brexit.

To keep its inefficient steel mills running, China shipped significant quantities of below-cost steel to the European Union (EU), a practice in international trade that is called dumping. The EU had, and has, legal remedies under the World Trade Organization (WTO) to prevent dumping. But the EU ignored the problem at first. At the time, Germany, which was enjoying major positive trade flows with China, deliberately stalled the EU's case against Chinese dumping at the WTO, out of fear that China would retaliate against the very profitable German products flooding into China. In retrospect the German position was shortsighted, but at the time it would have been politically imprudent within Germany to challenge China over steel dumping. In the long term, however, Germany's short-term political and economic expediency fueled a fire that would end up being much more detrimental to Germany and the EU than any possible trade retaliation from China.

China's dumping of massive quantities of steel free from any major action by the EU with the WTO ended up having a direct effect on the politics of the English Midlands and thus on the EU itself. Unlike the worker in Toledo, Ohio, that I wrote about in chapter 2, the jobs of the British steelworkers in the English Midlands were not being threatened by automation; they were being directly threatened by China's policy to support its own inefficient steel manufacturing industry. In 2012 the United Kingdom imported about fifty thousand metric tons of steel rebar from China. By 2015, however, that figure skyrocketed to four hundred thousand metric tons. The massive Chinese steel imports forced English steel mills to dramatically reduce their prices, causing further economic repercussions.

By stalling on an action to cite China in a WTO dumping case, the EU directly—but inadvertently—aided the antiglobalist forces gathering steam in the Midlands of England. The troubles in the English steel industry became another bullet in the Brexit gun. The irony here is that President Xi of China sees himself as the ultimate globalist. But the reality, as we have learned, is that globalism is a game that must be played delicately, and political protectionism at home in our age of globalization can rapidly become a political fire abroad.

In the United States, protectionism of course predates the age of Trump. Abraham Lincoln even owes his nomination to the presidency to it. Lincoln's new Republican Party was the handmaiden of the American industrial revolution. The party was formed by combining Lincoln's railroad supporters (the Apple and Google of their day) with northern abolitionism, then sprinkling them with the doctrine of "free man, free soil," which appealed to America's newly minted entrepreneurs.

In 1860, at the Wigwam convention in Chicago where Lincoln was nominated, the interest of the new industrialist were as important as abolitionist theory in putting together the first winnable Republican coalition. Lincoln and his advisers had calculatedly included a high-tariff plank in their first platform to ensure the votes for nomination of the then rapidly industrializing state of Pennsylvania.

Horace Greeley, publisher of the *New York Tribune*, the unofficial national newspaper of the new Republican Party, expressed the need for the tariff plank best when he said to an associate shortly before the Wigwam convention, "Now about the Presidency: I want to succeed this time, yet I know the country is not anti-slavery. It will only swallow a little anti-slavery in a great deal of sweetening. An anti-slavery man per se cannot be elected; but a tariff, river and harbor, Pacific Railroad, Free homestead man may succeed although he is anti-slavery."

There is, however, a major difference between the protectionism of Lincoln and the protectionist measures sponsored by the Trump administration and the antiglobalists. The purpose of Lincoln's measures was to shelter America's new industries, to give them a chance to grow free of more powerful foreign competitors. In stark contrast, the antiglobalist measures are to protect America's nonglobalized, dying industries.

Protectionism is also not new as a political placebo to pacify constituencies destroyed by technological changes. In its most benign form, it is like the historic Roman circus, distracting the population: a cheap political trick that when performed appears to have no cost to the constituency. The problem occurs when the political rhetoric of protectionism then forces shortsighted political action, passing the cost on to others without giving any thought of how that cost can ricochet with devastating impact. A concept first labeled by Adam Smith and then used by John Maynard Keynes called "beggar thy neighbor," it essentially involves taking a political action that economically might protect your country but makes your neighbor poorer.

The use of protectionism solely to politically pacify communities that cannot adapt to technological change, although easy to do in both democracies like the U.S. and autocracies like China, is a roadmap to disaster. The best example of this use brings us back to grain, as in the Corn Laws. In this case, however, it was not grain for human consumption but instead oats to feed horses.

In the early to mid-1920s the growing of horse feed in the United States, a major part of the American farm economy, was being battered by a massive technological change: the switch from horse-drawn vehicles to automobiles. As a common means of transportation, horses were rapidly becoming obsolete, and as a result the farmland dedicated to growing oats was no longer needed. It is estimated that one-sixth to one-quarter of all farmland cultivated in the United States before the automobile was dedicated to raising horse feed. With the advent of the automobile, that land was no longer needed for animal feed, and farmers across the United States planted crops for human consumption on what was previously oat fields. The resulting severe oversupply of food crops caused prices to fall, dramatically reducing farm income and making it difficult for farmers to pay the taxes and bank financing owed on their land. By the late 1920s, approximately 18 percent of American farms were in foreclosure.

The farmers at that time and their representatives in government advocated for an increase of tariffs on agricultural imports, similar to protecting coal or steel today. The numbers, however, showed no logical reason to increase agricultural tariffs. Most American farmers faced little competition from agricultural imports. In fact, the opposite was true: exports accounted for 15–17 percent of farm income in 1926–29. But whether logical or not, protection against change is the easiest of political arguments to sell. It is pure economic populism; the outsider is destroying our economy and must be prevented from doing so.

In his campaign for reelection in 1928, President Herbert Hoover, a Republican, promised to help the farmers by increasing tariffs on agriculture imports. After his successful reelection and with the Republican Party having comfortable majorities in both the Senate and the House of Representatives, Hoover asked Congress for an increase in tariffs on agricultural products.

With politics being politics, once the bill to raise tariffs on agricultural products—which would be known as the Smoot-Hawley Tariff Act—was introduced to Congress, the horse trading began. Naturally the senators and congressional representatives from the non-farm states traded their support for agricultural tariffs by demanding support for higher tariffs on manufactured products. By the time the Smoot-Hawley Act was finalized in Congress and sent to President Hoover for his signature, it imposed an effective tax rate of 60 percent on more than thirty-two hundred products and materials imported into the United States, quadrupling previous tariff rates on individual items.

It was clear to almost all the major economists in the United States at that time, as well as the leading industrialists and bankers, that Smoot-Hawley would lead to economic disaster. A petition signed by over one thousand leading economists was sent to President Hoover, asking him to veto the bill. Henry Ford and Thomas Edison pleaded with Hoover not to sign the bill, and Thomas Lamont, the head of J. P. Morgan, was quoted as saying that he "almost went down on [his] knees to beg Herbert Hoover to veto the asinine Hawley-Smoot tariff." Hoover ignored all of this advice and signed the bill.

Smoot-Hawley's disastrous impact on the United States and the world was immediate. The press in Belgium, Italy, France, Germany, Spain, Sweden, and Switzerland instantly went on the attack. In France, Smoot-Hawley was compared to a declaration of war, an economic blockade. In Sweden the popular press labeled it "the most terrible blow against the economic life of the world," while a newspaper in England compared it to the German attack of 1914.

Politically, there was nothing these countries could do to appease their own constituents' anger against Smoot-Hawley but double down on a "beggar thy neighbor strategy" and raise tariffs against U.S. products, in particular the auto industry. The U.S. auto industry was an easy target to retaliate against, since before Smoot-Hawley, American cars made up 54 percent of world trade in motor vehicles.

In Italy a royal decree that became effective ten days after President Hoover signed the Smoot-Hawley Tariff Act increased import duties on American automobiles substantially. Duties on less expensive American cars were doubled and raised even higher against the more expensive models. Previous to this decree, 80 percent of all Italian imports of automobiles originated in the United States. In Spain a new tariff schedule increased the rates on American automobiles, motorcycles, pneumatic tires, safety-razor blades, and sewing machines. The French also significantly increased their duties on American automobiles and parts.

In the category of "be careful what you wish for," U.S. farm exports after the passage of Smoot-Hawley dropped by a third between 1929 and 1933. Retaliation against U.S. cotton, for example, was immediate. Even American apples and eggs came under attack. Three days after the Smoot-Hawley bill became effective, Great Britain prohibited the importation of certain grades of raw apples from the United States, and Argentina imposed restrictions on the importation of American eggs. The severe decline in U.S. agricultural exports obviously made a troubled farm economy worse, forcing many farm banks in the Midwest and south to fail.

Economists differ on whether the Smoot-Hawley Tariff Act of 1930 was one of the main drivers of the Great Depression or merely an accessory to the crime. Obviously Smoot-Hawley could not have directly caused the stock market collapse of October 1929, since the tariff was not signed into law until the following June. As we now know, however, markets react to anticipated news. Just look at the run-up in the U.S. stock markets in 2017 in the anticipation of a corporate tax cut. Data also shows that banks, at the time Smoot-Hawley was being negotiated in Congress, stopped supporting exporters in anticipation of foreign reaction to the impending rise in U.S. tariffs.

On the other hand, noted economists such as Milton Friedman have argued that foreign trade was too small a percentage of the U.S. economy at the onset of Smoot-Hawley for it to be a major cause of the Depression. The problem with the Friedman theory, however, is that although exports accounted for only 7 percent of our national production in 1929, this figure was scattered across vital areas. So, for example, exports accounted for 15–17 percent of farm income in 1926–29, and as noted earlier that income was devastated by retaliation against Smoot-Hawley.

It is also normally assumed that only the retaliatory tariffs enacted against Smoot-Hawley by other countries caused the greatest harm to the American economy. But looking more deeply at the situation, Alan Reynolds of the Cato Institute points out that the Smoot-Hawley tariffs on imports had an equally negative effect, possibly foretelling a similar situation that could occur with our current sophisticated international integrated supply chain.

> Critical portions of the U.S. production process can be crippled by a high tax on imported materials. Other key industries are heavily dependent on exports. Disruptions in trade patterns then ripple throughout the economy. A tariff on linseed oil hurt the U.S. paint industry, a tariff on tungsten hurt steel, a tariff on casein hurt paper, a tariff on mica hurt electrical equipment, and so on. Over eight hundred things used in making automobiles were taxed by Smoot-Hawley. There were five hundred U.S. plants employing sixty thousand people to make cheap clothing out of imported wool rags; the tariff on wool rags rose by 140 per cent.

But whether Smoot-Hawley was a direct or indirect cause of the Great Depression or whether the decline in exports or the increased cost of imports hurt the U.S. economy obscures the main lesson of

Smoot-Hawley: raising tariffs to protect constituencies confronted by technological change leads to disaster. Smoot-Hawley is the grand example of a political placebo combined with the economics of passing the buck. We also need to keep in mind that Smoot-Hawley happened in 1930 during America's so-called "period of isolationism." One can only speculate how much greater the damage could be in a globalized world.

The political fight between the old fixed-asset-based industries and the new tech industries is similar to the Corn Laws fight mentioned earlier in another important way. The landed British aristocracy had a cultural problem understanding the new wealth created by what they called trade, people who made money by actually going into an office and working for it and not by inheriting it. Beyond aristocratic snobbishness, the fundamental understanding of each group's view of the other's economic assets and what was needed to make them profitable was totally divergent. The concept of mass production and factories was as foreign to the landed gentry as the idea of tenant farmers was to the factory owners. These were two different ways of life with different rhythms, different economic valuations, and different concepts of both investment and return.

Today's fight resonates across the same economic perceptual disconnects. Business is just not business, and depending on the industry, one's worldview is totally different. Jonathan Haskel and Stian Westlake describe it beautifully in their book *Capital without Capitalism*, where they discuss how intangible assets—whether software, manuals, or R and D—and not tangible, or fixed, assets, such as steel mills and coal mines, are now the leading areas of investment in the United States. As they stated, "It should come as no surprise that things that one can't touch, like ideas, commercial relationships, and know-how, are fundamentally different from physical things like machines and buildings."

Haskel and Westlake describe how an investment in an intangible such as Starbucks takes a mindset that is totally different from that for an investment in a steel mill. It is impossible to move steel mills (they truly are fixed), but as the authors point out, "Once you've written the Starbucks operating manual in Chinese—an investment

in organizational development—you can use it in each of the country's 1,200-plus stores." In fact Starbucks in 2017 had been opening
a new store in China every fifteen hours on average. And Starbucks
is a minor example of how the concept of the scalability of knowledge and the move to an intangible-asset economy has redefined
economic activity in a manner not so different from the divide
between pre- and post-industrial-revolution England.

Just look at Facebook's software, which can be scaled more or less
interminably, and compare it to Koch Industries and their investments in fixed assets: carbon-based chemicals, asphalt, and pulp
and paper plants. In fact, because of scalability, Facebook now has
more users in India than in any other country. And Google and
Facebook attracted one-fifth of global advertising spending in 2016,
nearly double the figure of five years ago.

Or look at retailing and Walmart versus Amazon. Walmart was the
dominant retailer in the United States, with its five thousand brick-
and-mortar stores, but it struggles now to compete with Amazon,
whose presence is easily accessible on everyone's cell phones. Walmart
was never truly a merchant but a master of the supply chain, getting bulk products from China to the United States more efficiently
than anyone else. Now, however, the company not only needs to figure out how to merchandize products but to do it over the internet.

The difference in approach between these two companies is revolutionary. Amazon will alert my phone to remind me that last year
I bought my nephew a certain gift for his birthday; now that he is
a year older, he might enjoy something else they are recommend-
ing. When has a Walmart store ever reminded anyone that they
needed to buy a birthday present and kept track of the previous gift
as well as the age of the recipient? And what happens to the huge
fixed investment that Walmart has in real estate?

These dissimilarities that are both cultural and economic are key
to understanding the struggle between the new industries and the old
for government support. But they also demonstrate why the zeitgeist
of the people involved in these industries is so radically different. If
scalability is important to one's return on investment, globalization
is a must, with one's political views absolutely leaning toward inter-

nationalism and globalism. On the other hand, if you are an investor or a worker in a steel mill that physically cannot scale, your interest lies in manufacturing at full capacity and preventing foreign competition from eating into your market. The scalable company is not fearful of domestic competition, and in fact in their world ideas are shared: what they want is unified fair global rules of trade. That is why such trade pacts as the TPP (Trans-Pacific Partnership)—which the Trump administration not only killed but constantly boasts about killing—are so important to the new industries.

Google, Microsoft, Apple, and Facebook lobbied furiously for TPP. The trade pact would have allowed these companies to more easily store user data across borders and enjoy stricter copyright protection while clamping down on digital piracy. It also included the world's first set of international trade rules that would have barred governments from blocking how companies share data across national borders. This provision was extremely important because if data can be blocked and can't be scaled—or, to use the industry term, "Balkanized"—then in a world of intangible investments the growth of these investments becomes limited. It is obvious that as in the earlier example of Boeing, a major determinant is the size of the market. For the intangible industries that can be scaled more or less ad infinitum, smaller markets with legal trade barriers are not only less attractive places to develop these industries but also detrimental to the growth of these industries.

All this leads directly back to the Crawleys of *Downton Abbey* fame. Even though the manufacturing facilities of the English industrial revolution were not scalable per se, their products were what the world wanted. It became fairly obvious that England as a whole would become much wealthier selling steam engines and steel to the world than by supporting an agricultural industry on an island not known for its sunlight or perfect growing conditions. And just as in England in the 1830s and 1840s but with the additional pressure of globalized social media, no matter how many political gyrations are performed to try to keep the old industries alive, the logic of globalization will apply.

FIVE

Becoming Less Great

I t has been said that John F. Kennedy would listen to the score of the Broadway musical *Camelot*, envisioning that his Washington would rise to the noblest deeds of the Arthurian legend. As it happens, Arthur's Round Table did come to America—not during the New Frontier but twenty-seven years later under a new name: globalization. And similar to what Alan Jay Lerner wrote in his bewitching lyrics for *Camelot*, the halcyon hopes of globalization appear to have lasted only for a "brief shining moment," before they gave way to a babel of national and global misunderstanding.

When the Berlin Wall came down in 1989, it appeared that a new world was approaching, a world far more similar to Arthur's Round Table than to the Cold War that just preceded it. Though written several years earlier, the lyrics for a Coca-Cola jingle, "I'd like to teach the world to sing in perfect harmony," became something of an unofficial anthem for the new world of globalization.

Europe was about to be reunited under a liberal democratic capitalist system. Russia looked as though it could possibly develop into a democratic capitalist country. The first Iraq war was still a year away, and few in the West or in the population centers of Asia were yet aware of the depth of the historic Sunni-Shia rivalry in the Middle East. And China—if not democratic—had turned toward capitalism, with its economy booming and a foreign policy based on Deng Xiaoping's saying "Take a low profile and never take the lead." In retrospect, this saying was not radically different from what

Theodore Roosevelt said when America was going through its own industrial revolution: "Speak softly and carry a big stick."

Just as *globalization* became the hot new buzzword, trade and dollar flows became the new conquering armies, breaking down borders in a way not seen since Caesar's time. Globalization even challenged the power of nation-states. By using the marketplace to vote on the validity of a country's fiscal condition, markets became the ultimate judges of a nation's economic wherewithal. In the process, globalization often usurped political power from a country's leadership. It was the time of George H. W. Bush's New World Order. Although fuzzy in its description, this concept implied a world working together to protect the rule of law, rather than one divided by divergent interests.

Francis Fukuyama, the political economist, referred to this unique time as "the end of history." Fukuyama did not mean that history itself had ended and that wars and conflicts would not occur anymore. What he meant was that liberal democracy had prevailed in the centuries-long ideological fight over which governmental system ultimately benefits its citizenry the best. Fukuyama made the prophetic observation that for those parts of the world that had reached "the end of history," economics would outstrip politics or military grand strategy in importance.

Trade figures show clearly how the world was changing. In 1989 total U.S. exports were $487 billion, though by 2000 the U.S. was exporting $1.075 trillion of goods and services. During the same period, U.S. exports to China alone went from $5.7 billion to $16.1 billion. At the same time, though, China's exports to the U.S. went from $11.9 billion to $100 billion. But it was not just China and the United States whose trade was exploding; the phenomenon was truly global. According to the World Bank, global trade in merchandise exports nearly doubled, rising from $3.5 trillion in 1990 to $6.2 trillion in 2001.

Chinese exports defined this new age of globalization and global trade. Though China was rapidly becoming the factory to the world, these factories at that time were essentially labor-intense assembly plants. The parts and raw materials for these factories came from all over the world. White leather athletic shoes, then a popular fashion item, offer an excellent example of globalized trade's complexity. These shoes were made in China by major brands like Nike, Adidas, and Puma. But the main component of the shoes—the leather—did not come from China, a land with a relatively small number of cattle. The leather itself was truly globalized. Most of the white leather used in the shoes originated as a product called crust, semifinished leather from Brazil or Argentina. The crust was shipped from South America to Johnstown in upstate New York, where it was finished and sprayed white. From Johnstown the now-white leather was put into containers and sent to China, to be made into shoes that eventually were sold in the malls of America.

This globalized process of China being the assembly factory to the world—but not at that time the true originator of the product—continued as Chinese production moved up in the product cycle. Consider the iPhone as an example. Only about ten dollars of its total cost is attributed to assembly in China. The majority of its parts come from all over the world, with the actual product design, software development, management, and marketing coming from the United States.

When Bill Clinton came into office in 1993, he expanded on the George H. W. Bush administration's concept of a new world order. Although primarily concentrating on domestic affairs, the Clinton administration saw the new age of globalization as a net positive for the United States. Clinton—the ultimate pragmatist—had what the Germans call *fingerspitzengefühl*, a sense of things on one's fingertips, or as the dictionary describes it, great situational awareness. He instinctively understood how to ride the wave of history and perceived that globalization was the force of the future. As *Foreign Policy* stated on November 19, 2009,

> Bill Clinton understood sooner, better, and more profoundly than many other leaders that globalization was not simply a trendy buzzword. [As Clinton stated in a speech in Los Angeles on February 27, 1999,] "Everything from the strength of our economy to the safety of our cities to the health of our peo-

ple depends on events not only within our borders but half a world away."

Clinton's tenure has coincided with a historic convergence of technological and political trends (the Internet, democratization, open markets, and porous borders) that facilitated an unprecedented level of global integration. Not content to let the United States be carried along by the currents and tides of globalization, Clinton sought to accelerate and harness these forces and mitigate their volatility. He led intense efforts to lower trade and investment barriers—completing the North American Free Trade Agreement (NAFTA) with Canada and Mexico, concluding the Uruguay Round of the General Agreement on Tariffs and Trade (GATT), supporting the creation of the World Trade Organization (WTO), and urging Congress to pass the African Growth and Opportunity Act. As AIDS and other infectious diseases spread throughout developing nations, the White House pressed the World Bank and industrialized countries to increase public health funding. The White House also made the environment a high priority, creating a new under secretary for global affairs at the State Department and better integrating environmental issues into its foreign-policy planning.

Economic and political globalization were the new dynamic change agents of the post–Cold War world. But for historical change to become successfully embedded in global political culture, it must be sanctified by the leading power of the time. This requirement has been true throughout history, whether it was the Roman emperor Constantine's acceptance of Christianity or the U.S. blessing the economic integration of western Europe through the Marshall Plan. The power of the hegemon to be the role model and to accept change becomes integral to the success of the change.

The contrary is also true; if the hegemon walks away and does not support the new changes, those changes have a far greater chance of withering. A prime example of this rule is when the U.S. Senate, on November 19, 1919, rejected the Treaty of Versailles to end World War I by a vote of thirty-nine to fifty-five, and in the process rejecting U.S. membership in the new League of Nations and its system of collective security. Although the League of Nations was certainly imperfectly structured at its inception, by walking away from the League, the United States flatly stated it had no responsibility for global security. This was despite the fact that nearly 117,000 Americans died and 204,000 were wounded fighting in World War I, and despite the fact that by that time America had become an economic hegemon as the world's largest industrial nation. Interestingly, it was the first time the U.S. Senate had ever rejected a peace treaty. While the vote rejecting the treaty was based partly on a misreading of the politics of the U.S. Senate by President Wilson and partly on America's cultural tendency toward fear of the outside world, the results were historic. It indirectly added another cause of World War II, which happened less than twenty years later.

If not fully walking away from globalization, America's fear of loss of sovereignty on account of globalization, in a sense fearing not being singularly in control of world events, became the underpinnings of America's foreign policy. Theodore Roosevelt supposedly said, "In any moment of decision, the best thing you can do is the right thing, the next best thing is the wrong thing, and the worst thing you can do is nothing." In terms of nurturing the new era of globalization, the administration of George W. Bush combined the last two attributes of Roosevelt's saying. They did the wrong thing, which then by their actions implied that the U.S. would do nothing politically to recognize, organize, and support the changes in the world that were occurring on account of globalization. It is important to note that the George W. Bush administration was not against the United States being involved in the world. It was not isolationist; in fact it was quite the opposite. It just failed to see the reality of globalization. Trying to turn the United States back to isolationism when its economy and the world were already globalized had to wait until Donald Trump was elected president.

It is difficult for any leader to read history and judge how his or her acts will positively or negatively affect the future. Several factors are critical: the leader's personality, the culture they were raised in, their political temperament, and their reading of the nation's political climate. While the Clinton administration was extremely prescient in seeing globalization as a new force of history that the United States should harness and ride, the Bush administration saw it as a threat to American exceptionalism. They saw globalization as an attack on the new singular hegemonic power that the United States gained at the end of the Cold War. Although not as headline-building or humanly tragic as the administration's misjudgment on Iraq, Bush's misreading of how the world had evolved—and thus on whether to negate globalization or harness it—is of equal historic importance.

Globalization was antithetical to the Bush administration's neo-conservative value of American exceptionalism. Many in the administration thought President George H. W. Bush's New World Order had been naive in its worldview. This new Bush administration focused instead on protecting U.S. interests and guaranteeing future U.S. economic security and superiority. Philosophically, it could not tolerate the slow erosion of the power of the nation-state that was implicit as globalization sped forward.

The policies and theories for the George W. Bush administration's views on America's role in the world began to take root several years before the administration actually came into office. At a think tank called the Project for a New American Century (PNAC), established in 1997 by two of the leading neoconservatives of the time, William Kristol and Robert Kagan, the mantra was America as the sole surviving hegemon, not globalization. The PNAC's founding statement of principles read: "As the 20th century draws to a close, the United States stands as the world pre-eminent power. Having led the West to victory in the Cold War, America faces an opportunity and a challenge: Does the United States have the vision to build upon the achievements of past decades? Does the United States have the resolve to shape a new century favorable to American principles and interests?"

Of course, there are many think tanks in Washington offering philosophical positions on every subject one could imagine, but what made the PNAC different was that its original signers would later have the power to aggressively act on its theories. Dick Cheney, the future vice president in the George W. Bush administration, as well as Donald Rumsfeld, the future secretary of defense, and Paul Wolfowitz, the future undersecretary of defense, were among the twenty-five people who signed the PNAC's founding statement.

Several attempts were made during George H. W. Bush's term in office to translate neoconservative geopolitical ideology into public policy. Paul Wolfowitz, at that time undersecretary of defense for policy, and his deputy Scooter Libby, who would become chief of staff to Vice President Dick Cheney, wrote a forty-six-page draft policy statement for the Defense Department. Its basic principle was that in the post–Cold War world, no power should be able to rival the United States. In its leaked version it stated that part of America's goal would be "convincing potential competitors that they need not aspire to a greater role or pursue a more aggressive posture to protect their legitimate interests." Further stating that, the U.S. "must maintain the mechanisms for deterring potential competitors from even aspiring to a larger regional or global role."

The document made no reference to collective action, a cornerstone of America's post–World War II policy. It also didn't grasp that economic power was now part of the game.

When leaked, the draft caused a severe uproar within the administration. It was so contrary in principle to many of the policies of the first Bush administration that Colin Powell, then chairman of the Joint Chiefs of Staff, quickly supervised a rewrite.

With the inauguration of George W. Bush in January 2001, what was once a think tank's theory in international relations and defense postures was now put into definitive practice. With Cheney, Rumsfeld, and Wolfowitz now in power, the Pentagon's Office of Net Assessment published an eighty-five-page monograph titled "Military Advantage in History" in the summer of 2002. This time there was no backlash and no rewrite supervised by a pragmatist like Colin Powell. The purpose of this monograph was to look at why empires lasted over time or failed. The study looked at four empires, what the study called "pivotal hegemonic powers in history, to examine how the U.S. could maintain its advantage in the 21st century."

Before the study was even published, however, the Bush administration very publicly demonstrated its go-it-alone approach to the world, including the discontinuation of treaties that the administration believed would hold the United States back. Since John Kennedy's time, treaties between the Soviet Union and the United States limiting nuclear weapons and missiles were a key part of American foreign policy, practically sacrosanct. On December 13, 2001, the Bush administration disregarded that precedent and gave Russia notice that it was withdrawing from the Anti-Ballistic Missile (ABM) Treaty, which the United States had signed with the Soviet Union in 1972.

On nullifying the treaty with Russia, President Bush stated, "I have concluded the ABM treaty hinders our government's ways to protect our people from future terrorist or rogue state missile attacks." In retrospect, of course, a ballistic missile could be considered a weapon that is far too complex and expensive for terrorist groups, making it an extremely inefficient means of wreaking havoc. Bush went on to state, "Defending the American people is my highest priority as commander in chief, and I cannot and will not allow the United States to remain in a treaty that prevents us from developing effective defenses."

The Bush administration's action did, however, give further credence to a psychologically distraught Russia for its soon-to-be full retreat from globalization. Vladimir Putin had become the president of the Russian Federation approximately one year before George W. Bush took office. Putin's primary problem was dealing with a Russian economy that had come close to anarchy. In foreign policy, he saw his role as reasserting Russia as a credible power. Certainly as a sixteen-year veteran of the KGB who resigned in 1991 with the rank of lieutenant colonel, he had to be angered and aggrieved by the Soviet Union's collapse, as well as the expansion of NATO into the former Soviet satellites. But he also wanted, using novelist John le Carré's words, to bring Russia "in from the cold," to connect Russia to the rest of the world, and to become a full partner in global relations.

September 11, 2001, had given Putin both a public and a private opportunity to do that. When the World Trade Towers were attacked,

Putin was the first foreign leader to call President Bush to offer help, saying later on Russian TV, "Russia knows directly what terrorism means, and because of this we, more than anyone, understand the feelings of the American people. In the name of Russia, I want to say to the American people—we are with you."

The help that Putin gave to the United States was unprecedented in the history of the relations between the two countries. Intelligence information Russia had on the infrastructure in Afghanistan, and the location of terrorists within that country, was handed over to the Americans. Putin then acquiesced to open Russian airspace for American planes going to Afghanistan and coordinated with the former Soviet Central Asian republics for America to use former Soviet military bases. In addition, supplies for American troops in Afghanistan were transported through Russia.

Given these examples, it is easy to understand Putin's dismay when President Bush abrogated the ABM treaty. In a nationwide TV address the same day Bush tore up the treaty, Putin said that "the treaty is a cornerstone of world security and the decision to withdraw was an erroneous one."

The problem with Russia and the missiles, however, only intensified. In 2002 the Bush administration began talks with Poland and the Czech Republic about setting up a European base to intercept long-range missiles. The United States said the purpose of these bases would be to stop long-range missiles from Iran and the Middle East. The Russians naturally perceived these proposed bases as Cold War–like encirclement and threatened to put short-range nuclear missiles on the Polish border and on their borders with other NATO countries. Putin warned that this could be the start of a new cold war.

In a 2010 cable leaked by WikiLeaks, it became apparent that Poland wanted the missile shield on their territory because they felt threatened more by Russia than by Iran. When the U.S. proposed to Poland a more limited shield, Poland wanted assurances that the new plan could deal with "hypothetical threats."

Whether this missile shield was designed to protect the United States and its allies from Iranian or Russian rockets, or both, it was a plan based more on the ideology of the PNAC than the realities of the world. The Obama administration later halted the construction of the bases and issued a statement in September 2009, stating the U.S. "no longer planned to move forward with this project." In diplomatic language, it was rather easy to read through: the Obama White House said that new intelligence had shown Iran was pursuing short-range and medium-range missile development rather than long-range, which consequently would require a shift in strategy.

The year 2002 was also when President Bush backed an expansion of NATO to include the former Soviet republics of Latvia, Estonia, and Lithuania, as well as Romania, Slovakia, and Slovenia, all of which were admitted in 2004. In retrospect, after Putin's Crimea annexation in 2014, allowing the Baltic nations to join NATO looks like a very wise and prescient move. But one could also seriously speculate about historic causation and whether the failure to appreciate Putin's opening to the West in the early years of the Bush administration led Putin—based on his background—to see an evil that did not exist. As Thomas E. Graham, who served as Bush's senior director for Russia on the National Security Council, later said, "We never tested Putin. Our policy never tested Putin to see whether he was really committed to a different type of relationship."

It was not just on defense issues that the Bush administration was dictating a policy of singularity and exceptionalism. On March 28, 2001, the Bush administration effectively ended any chance of the Kyoto international treaty on global climate change having credibility as a global governing document when it withdrew the U.S. signature from the accord. The treaty was the first international attempt to slow down the emission of greenhouse gasses. Clinton's vice president, Al Gore, had signed the Kyoto accord on behalf of the U.S. on November 12, 1998, but the Senate never ratified it. Without the backing of the United States—the hegemon, which also at the time was the world's largest energy consumer—the Kyoto treaty was largely ineffective.

Kyoto was about more than global climate change. It was a statement that the world had become interconnected, and with it the recognition that environmental issues now had the power to pierce sovereign borders and damage nation-states in a manner somewhat similar to that of old-fashioned disputes over territories and ideology. With the rejection of Kyoto, the Bush administration sent a clear signal that the United States, the liberal hegemon, would not go along with the new world order. Any concept that would limit what the administration perceived as America's domestic or international advantages would be rejected, no matter how short-term any gain from those advantages proved to be. It was a clear signal that the administration did not understand the difference between maintaining a short-term advantage and giving up some of that advantage to be the leader in the emerging globalized world. The world was shifting rapidly, and instead of reorienting American policy—both internationally and domestically—to harness and lead that change, the Bush administration insisted on still viewing the world through the prism of an American hegemonic empire. And of course with what we now know about global climate change this was a tremendous error.

Fifteen years later, looking back on the Bush administration's decision to forgo Kyoto, Liam Downey and Timmons Roberts wrote in a July 7, 2016, blog of the Brookings Institution:

By 2001, when George W. Bush took office, there was scientific consensus on the seriousness of climate change, ample evidence of the perils of petro-politics, and nearly two decades of experience with renewable and energy efficiency technologies.—It is therefore important to remember and learn from such a key moment in history when our political and economic leaders had an opportunity to join Japan and Europe in turning sharply toward efficiency, conservation and renewable energy, or to double down on fossil fuels. Unfortunately, the Bush administration made a devastating choice: rather than leading the world to a greener future, the Bush White House set the U.S. and the world back 15 years in their attempts to rein in the climate crisis.

Combined with the abrogation of the ABM treaty, American disregard for Kyoto was an unmistakable signal to the world that the United States was not at all interested in legally maintaining and establishing any new international legal precedents to guide globalization, in fact just the opposite. Senator Edward M. Kennedy described the Bush actions, as well as the concept behind them that became known as the Bush Doctrine, as "a call for 21st century American imperialism that no other nation can or should accept."

Ironically, much of the shift in the global balance, which the Bush administration failed to perceive, was created by post–World War II American policy. At the end of the war, America's military and economic might were at commanding heights. America was the singular liberal hegemon, the leading nation with the ability and will to set the global economic agenda, to be the global policeman. And in principle—with some slight detours—that is exactly what it did almost from the end of the war. For example, in Europe the Truman administration conditioned NATO on Germany and France coming together to form the European Steel and Coal Community, an early forerunner of the European Union. And in the administration that followed, Eisenhower threatened in 1954 an "agonizing reappraisal" of the U.S. commitment to Europe if Europe did not further integrate.

In its role as the liberal hegemon, America became something unusual: the nurturing mother. American rules were simple: as long as a country was aligned with the United States against Soviet communism, America would encourage and support its economic growth and protect its international trade. It made no difference whether a country was a democracy. "Semidemocratic" South Korea and Taiwan received our support, as did China after Nixon's visit in 1972.

Never before had the leading power purposely worked to share the formula for its wealth, or behaved as if its mission was the creation of a democratic and capitalist world of plenty. Yet this is exactly what America has very successfully done over the past sixty-five years.

The U.S. policy during the post–World War II years included a mandate to create a world full of opportunities that would lift other nations up on a rising tide of democracy, capitalism, and entrepreneurialism.

As the countries under America's economic umbrella became economic giants themselves, two forces collided, leading us to the blindman's bluff of rulemaking that we are facing today. First, as these newly economically empowered countries grew, they logically demanded their right to have a say in global rulemaking. Consequently, America's hegemonic power—its ability to be the prime rule maker—began to recede. Second, and almost concurrently, the new force of globalization was emerging, putting into high relief the dilution of the sovereignty of states. Countries became less effective at regulating their own economies. Their ability to defend their citizens against global terrorism, disease, and global climate change declined.

The cocktail of modern globalization has two main components, economic and political, which are then shaken together by the new forces of technology. The components play off local cultures, while also affecting them. The downside of this, however, is if left unchecked and unmanaged, economic globalization is similar to laissez-faire economics. Capital on its own will disregard any human concern to find the best possible return. And once it became easy for capital to jump national borders, its power increased exponentially. But capital that is properly harnessed creates tremendous economic growth. As Bill Clinton said in February 1993, "We cannot repeal international economic competition. We can only harness the energy to our benefit."

Harnessing it, however, implies political foresight and action. It also implies that a country's leadership understands it must give up some area of sovereignty to facilitate growth and stability in an interconnected world. As an example, Germany and the other EU countries transitioned to relying on the data protection rules of the European Union, rather than their own national regulations in this area. Similarly, China relaxed and changed over seven thousand tariffs and quotas upon its entry into the World Trade Organization. Of course, this kind of progress can't be done without leadership that understands how the world has changed.

The Bush administration didn't perceive that by rejecting the political component of globalization, the ability to harness and direct it, they would be allowing the economic component to go unchecked. And that they were giving a signal similar to the one given when the United States rejected the League of Nations: that the world had not and could not change. In their minds, it was still a world of realpolitik, where countries acted purely for their self-interest, rather than a globalized world where the political and economic health of other leading nations directly affected the health and security of the United States. The Bush administration was frankly stating that they saw the world not as a globalized environment but as a go-it-alone world where each country would—and should—act for its own self-interest.

What is particularly interesting about the Bush administration's view is that it appears to have been purely ideological, and not forced on the administration by any form of pragmatic political pressure. At the time, there was little discussion of the economic effects of globalization on American industry, or about job losses resulting from outsourcing. These problems were hidden from sight, first by the information technology boom of the 1990s and later by the housing boom.

Obviously, the Bush administration was keenly aware of some of the economic components of globalization, both from the increased trade flows and what had become a symbiotic relationship between the United States' deficit and the Chinese ownership of a good portion of that debt. Fortunately for the administration, China's enormous purchases of U.S. debt had not yet become a real political issue, along with the fact the inflow of capital from China was a tremendous boost to the administration's domestic economic program.

As the *New York Times* editorialized on October 23, 2006,

> The Chinese sell a lot of merchandise in the United States and, in the process, accumulate a lot of dollars. They then loan many of those dollars back to the United States in exchange for all manner of American i.o.u.'s, including Treasury bonds, federal agency bonds, and private-sector debt.
>
> America's indebtedness to China, as a result, is staggeringly high, although the Bush administration—which needs foreign

loans to help finance the budget deficit—seems unfazed. But there is reason for pause. The *Wall Street Journal* reported this week that China's holdings of foreign currency and securities would soon top $1 trillion, a fivefold increase since 2000. Roughly 70 percent of that is believed to be in dollars or dollar-based assets.

For several years, China's loans have helped to keep prices and interest rates low in the United States, and to finance big tax cuts. If the lending began to dry up—because Chinese officials decided to diversify into other currencies or to spend more at home—prices, interest rates and taxes in the United States would very likely rise.

The Bush administration just didn't see—or didn't want to see—the link between economic and political globalization. Bush administration officials firmly believed in the economic theory that markets are self-regulating, so it follows that money flowing around the world should be the same. Furthermore, for practitioners of a foreign policy based on a concept of strict American hegemony, combined with a Wilsonian drive to make the world safe for democracy, the idea that markets could now be a new source of power or have as much power as a country did not fit into their worldview. What the administration didn't understand was that as the world was becoming more globalized, every international political signal by the hegemon could also have economic implications.

There are probably hundreds of cultural and psychological reasons why the Clinton administration was able to see globalization as the future while the George W. Bush administration was trapped in a myopic fantasy of an American empire. Several historians have written, as an example, that Lyndon Johnson, a child of Munich and World War II, had difficulty separating his formative experiences from the reality that Vietnam might not necessarily lead to the domino effect. Such an analogy, however, is difficult to apply to Bush and Clinton, since both were brought up during the same period and in fact Bush had the advantage of a father who was an internationalist. The difference appears to be Clinton's pragmatic reading of the world, as opposed to Bush trying to fit the world into an ideology.

The Bush administration's ideology, combined with the shock of 9/11 and the need to put that disaster into a frame of reference both to reassure domestic audiences and to clarify their response, clearly appears to have blinded the president and his cabinet. And for them, a frame of reference just happened to already exist. Eight years earlier, Professor Samuel Huntington, director of Harvard's Center for International Affairs, had begun looking at how the United States fit in the new post–Cold War world, and what the realities of globalization were. He described his worldview first in a lecture at the American Enterprise Institute, and then in the lead article in the summer 1993 issue of *Foreign Affairs*, titled "The Clash of Civilizations." The article was followed by his book *The Clash of Civilizations and the Remaking of World Order* in 1996.

In his post–Cold War worldview, Huntington saw neither a globalized world nor a world of realpolitik but a world of rival cultures. As he stated in the *Foreign Affairs* essay: "It is my hypothesis that the fundamental source of conflict in this new world will not be primarily ideological or primarily economic. The great divisions among humankind and the dominating source of conflict will be cultural. Nation states will remain the most powerful actors in world affairs, but the principal conflicts of global politics will occur between nations and groups of different civilizations. The clash of civilizations will dominate global politics. The fault lines between civilizations will be the battle lines of the future."

He went on to say, "During the cold war the world was divided into the First, Second and Third Worlds. Those divisions are no longer relevant. It is far more meaningful now to group countries not in terms of their political or economic systems or in terms of their level of economic development but rather in terms of their culture and civilization."

The Clash of Civilization theory was in many ways tailor-made for the horror of 9/11. It enabled the attack to be simply understood, putting it into a wider historic context for both Washington policy makers and the American public. Huntington's worldview, however, differed from that of the Bush administration in one major respect. Huntington believed that U.S. foreign policy had to be gentler, recognizing the differences in culture and history. Wisely, he urged restraint when it came to U.S. intervention.

The problem with Huntington's Clash is that it was looking at only part of the story, one level of a many-level world. Certainly, culture is a major determinant in human affairs and should not be ignored, but it is not the only determinant. Economics, the speed and fear of change, political leadership, climate, and many other factors are important variables that determine the behavior of nations.

In 2005, nine years after Huntington published his book and four years after 9/11, Thomas L. Friedman wrote *The World Is Flat*. The book was a clarion call to America to wake up to both the industrial changes and the global competition brought on by globalization. *The World Is Flat* was about economics and industrial policy, and it reflected Fukuyama's earlier idea that the world would be as preoccupied with economics as it was with politics.

Friedman's book became an instant best seller, it was a clarion call to America that globalization was a fact and we need to reorient our worldview and economy to take it into account. Fareed Zakaria described Friedman's ultimate question in his review of *The World Is Flat* for the *New York Times* on May 1, 2005: "The ultimate challenge for America—and for Americans—is whether we are prepared for this flat world, economic and political. While hierarchies are being eroded and playing fields leveled as other countries and people rise in importance and ambition, are we conducting ourselves in a way that will succeed in this new atmosphere? Or will it turn out that, having globalized the world, the United States had forgotten to globalize itself?"

What was strange, however, was how isolated the White House was from the reaction to the publication of *The World Is Flat*, especially since the White House's prime supporters, the American business community, were devouring the book. Almost immediately after publication of the book, every leading talk show and journal in the United States began talking about globalization. Many universities required *The World Is Flat* for freshman reading, and corporations added it as a component of their executive seminars. Even leading law journals ran articles about its implications for international law and international tax law. And Goldman Sachs and the *Financial Times* named *The World Is Flat* the business book of the year. The discussion permeated all levels of corporate activity. For example, the business journal *CIO* featured an article titled "What *The World Is Flat* Means to IT Outsourcing," while *Knowledge at Wharton*, the online journal of the Wharton School of the University of Pennsylvania, ran a major article titled "What Does It Take to Compete in a Flat World?" Strangely, however, it appears that the administration didn't have their TV sets on, or read any business journals. They didn't see that there was a disconnect between their foreign policy and what was going on in the business community; that under their leadership America was not guiding or leading the changes that were happening in the world on account of globalization. To the contrary, it was ignoring them.

Friedman's view was in many ways more prescient than Huntington's. Huntington, however, several years even before *The World Is Flat* was published, sarcastically ridiculed the basic concept of cultural and economic globalization. In an essay titled "The West Unique: Not Universal for Foreign Affairs" in November 1996, he stated, "The essence of Western civilization is the Magna Carta, not the Magna Mac." The same year Huntington wrote in his book *The Clash of Civilizations and the Remaking of World Order*, "Somewhere in the Middle East a half-dozen young men could well be dressed in jeans, drinking Coke, listening to rap, and between their bows to Mecca, putting together a bomb to blow up an American airliner."

Huntington's Mac sarcasm and his Mecca analogy were off. Globalization is not—and never has been—akin to the Magna Carta; instead it is an economic and social process. It has little to do with the Magna Carta idea of government; just look at little Singapore. And plotting to blow up a plane in the Middle East is psychologically more complex than Huntington acknowledges, and definitely doesn't emerge solely from inherently different cultures. China—in many ways the poster child of globalization success—has a radically different culture from the Western tradition that led to the Magna Carta. Yet despite the vast cultural difference, China does not have people blowing up airliners. In fact, China's early success at globalization had become a role model. Looking at the contrast between China and Egypt several years later, during the brief period of the Arab Spring, shows how the Huntington theory, which the Bush administration more or less hung their hats on, was just too simple.

China and Egypt, arguably the two oldest countries—if not nation-states—in the world, have a broadly similar history. Both were major empires in ancient times, and both were able to stay geographically and somewhat culturally intact over the centuries. Equally important, although both countries were severely manipulated by colonial powers during the past two hundred years, neither country fell completely under colonial rule for any long period. And in the years immediately after the Second World War, both countries were very poor. China in 1950 had a per capita domestic product of $614, while Egypt's was $514. Finally, both have had uprisings led by politically frustrated young people, China in Beijing's Tiananmen Square in 1989 and Egypt in Cairo's Tahrir Square in 2011.

But while Tiananmen Square was a call for more inclusive democracy as China's economy was growing substantially, Tahrir Square was about why Egypt's economy was only a little better in 2011 than it was after World War II. Young Egyptians, with the advent of the internet and cable, had seen the Olympic Games in Beijing in 2008 and contrasted China's success with their own nation's situation. These young Egyptians had to say to themselves, "Something isn't right." If China could rise up to economically challenge the United States, then what was wrong with their own country? Why were their lives so much more impoverished? Since Tiananmen Square, China had developed into the second-largest economy in the world, while Egypt, with its almost Brezhnevian-style leadership, continued to wallow in the past.

And that difference—the fact that a non-Western country, one almost as economically despondent as Egypt was only forty years ago, could now successfully challenge the West economically—was the siren song that Egyptians were listening to on Al Jazeera and the internet.

Revolting for a better life is slightly different from protesting for pure freedom. If you believe that, like you, everyone lives in a shack with a tin roof over it, then you are more accepting of your situation. But if, through the internet or social media, you can now see someone from another culture or country—that you thought was similar to yours—traveling on a bullet train while people in your country are still traveling by donkey cart, you begin to think something is wrong.

Sadly, the Arab Spring in Egypt failed, and although there was an amorphous call for freedom as part of the Cairo demonstrations, it was not necessarily a call to be identified with American or Huntington's values of freedom. This did not mean that globalization was not happening; it just meant that globalization and democracy are not necessarily synonymous.

Ironically, in 2017 Huntington's clash of civilizations was given a new life as part of the counterrevolution and antiglobalist manifesto. Just as its theories had been easily used by the Bush administration to put 9/11 into some form of historical context reborn, they were now being used to justify both an America First policy and one of Islamophobia. Of course, as in most manifestos, practicality and facts are sacrificed for theory. The reality is Huntington just doesn't work as a simplified one-size-fits-all policy. Throughout history the clash had little to do with civilizations and more to do with the shortsighted, arrogant, and paternalistic view of the world by Western or other leading cultures. Essentially, the most powerful nation of the time failed to appreciate, respect, or understand how its actions might be threatening and lead to future political problems in other nations.

Consider the situation of Iran, where long before the CIA-backed coup in 1953 overthrew the democratically elected Mossadegh government, the British had planted seeds that would grow into extreme distrust of the West.

In his monumental book *The Silk Roads: A New History of the World*, Peter Frankopan, director of the Oxford Centre for Byzantine Research, discusses background of this simmering mistrust in writing that in 1901, the UK essentially bribed its way into having the shah of Iran sign over the majority of rights to Iran's oil wealth.

The discovery of oil made the piece of paper signed by the Shah in 1901 one of the most important documents of the twentieth century. For while it laid the basis for a multi-billion-dollar business to grow—the Anglo-Persian Oil Company eventually became British Petroleum—it also paved the way for political turmoil. That the terms of the agreement handed control of Persia's crown jewels to foreign investors led to a deep and festering hatred of the outside world, which in turn led to nationalism and, ultimately, to a more profound suspicion and rejection of the west best epitomized in modern Islamic fundamentalism. The desire to win control of oil would be the cause of many problems in the future.

Frankopan goes on to talk about Central Southwest Asia seventy-eight years later, after the fall of the shah in 1979. He points out that the realpolitik needs of the major powers—in this case the United States—had as much to do with the clash of cultures that Huntington describes as the actual differences in the cultures.

Without mentioning Huntington, Frankopan's history of the Silk Roads effectively weakens much of Huntington's argument.

The fall of the Shah had set an extraordinary chain of events in motion. By the end of 1980, the whole of the centre of Asia was in a state of flux. The futures of Iran, Iraq and Afghanistan lay in the balance, resting on choices made by their leaders and on the intervention of outside forces. Guessing which way things would go in each of these countries let alone in the region as a whole was nigh on impossible. For the United States, the answer was to try to muddle through by playing all sides. The results were disastrous: while it was true that the seeds of anti-American sentiment had been planted earlier in the twentieth century, it was by no means inevitable that these would grow into full-blooded hatred. But U.S. policy decisions over the last two decades of the century would serve to poison attitudes across the region lying between the Mediterranean and the Himalayas.

Huntington aside, between 1989 and 2008, the world had changed practically overnight from the Cold War to the era of globalization. No longer split by two opposing economic and political spheres of communism and capitalism, the world appeared to be moving into one sphere, economically if not politically. But the failure of American government at that time to bless the change and lead politically would be, if not the end of Camelot, at least the beginning of what appeared to be the end. Simply put, an American policy of hegemonic dominance could not—and did not—work in an age of economic and technological globalization. By pursuing such a policy, the Bush administration not only lost its credibility but also sacrificed America's ability to shape a more cohesive world.

Nationalism begets nationalism, especially when sponsored by the hegemon. And when the United States made the determination that its interests could be better served with a unilateral strategy, it implicitly sanctioned the rights of other countries to withdraw from the round table. In subtle and not so subtle ways, other nations began to understand that it could now be beneficial to their own interests to discourage the centripetal forces of globalization.

This is not to say, for example, that Putin's worldview can be traced directly to the actions of the Bush administration; that is surely not the case. What the Bush administration's actions did was to establish that a nineteenth-century view of the world was still acceptable, and that although the United States was the victor in the Cold War, it would not put its power and prestige on the line to support any type of politically globalized integration.

The changes globalization made to sovereignty, economies, and individual livelihoods would invariably have produced some global backlash, as traditional cultural fault lines were being threatened, but it could have been mitigated if the American hegemon had used its influence and power to accept globalization, channel it, and even try to institutionalize it as the Obama administration later tried to do with the Paris climate agreement. Instead global nationalism began to slowly simmer, turning into a full-fledged fire fed by the economic crisis of 2008 and leading to the election of Donald Trump and his outright appeals to nativism and isolationism in the United States.

Misreading historic opportunities is certainly a sign of failure in leadership. And, for sure, the George W. Bush administration is guilty of that failure. There is a striking difference between the Bush administration's realpolitik view of American power and the populist isolationist view of the Trump administration. But if there is one major commonality between the two, it is a failure to comprehend that globalization has changed how the United States is now integrated with the world and that globalization is not a threat to the United States but instead plays to America's advantages. To overtly base U.S. policy, both domestic and foreign, on denying the integrating forces of globalization is truly not so different from the Austrian emperor Francis I in the 1900s refusing to build a northern railroad in the Austro-Hungarian empire for fear of change.

Since the early 1900s America's role in the world was predicated on the size of its economy. But that role was based on the fact that for all intents and purposes national economies were isolated; globalization has changed that and to change that back would be impossible. The next chapter, which I call "We Have Nothing to Fear but Fear Itself," looks at these changes and how they, along with technological disruption and misguided leadership, have caused us to doubt who we are.

SIX

We Have Nothing to Fear but Fear Itself

What happens when you apply Moore's Law not only to computer chips but to changes in industrial production and the sociopolitical fallout from those changes? Moore's Law, formulated by Gordon Moore of the Intel Corporation around 1970, stated that processor speeds, or overall processing power for computers, would double every two years.

Yet if machines can double their processing speed every two years or less (in fact, Moore's theory of doubling in two years has now become outdated, as processing speed has essentially become a self-propelling reality), how do humans adapt to the rapidity of that change?

In 2011 the *Smithsonian* magazine pointed out, "When faced with transformational technologies, people are afraid of losing things: cultural identities, ways of life, or economic security." For sure this phenomenon is not new; it is a recurring pattern throughout history. This fear of loss naturally generates political movements spurred by a combination of individuals who find it difficult to adjust and vested interests whose continued hold on power is threatened.

As an example, consider one of the greatest technological and cultural disrupters in Western civilization: the invention of movable type by Johannes Gutenberg in Germany in 1439. One can draw a direct line from Gutenberg's invention to Martin Luther, the Protestant Reformation, and the end of the Roman Catholic Church's political and cultural monopoly on power in Europe, as well as the advent of modern capitalism. But this same reformation brought about what we now call the Counter-Reformation: the fight by the Catholic Church, as well as other vested interests that benefited from the Church's power, to maintain its dominant position within Europe.

The invention of movable type and the printing press ended the Church's monopoly on information, especially on religious ideas that the Church thought were heretical or could challenge the Church's authority. The printing press enabled Martin Luther to become the first modern "tweeter," by means of pamphleteering. By 1521, Luther, essentially a previously unknown monk, had become an instant Renaissance celebrity and the most published author in Europe at the time, with 4,160 original essays that were ultimately republished in 828 editions. With Luther's sophisticated use of the new technology, the printing press, to criticize the church and distribute his theological writings across Europe, the Catholic doctrine of allowing only the clergy to read sacred documents fell as quickly as the biblical walls of Jericho.

The Counter-Reformation, which became the dominant—and in most cases, negative—force throughout Europe in the sixteenth and seventeenth centuries, directly caused the Thirty Years' War, which laid waste to much of central Europe. It also authorized the reestablishment of the Inquisition, persecuting—in some cases, via execution by burning—anyone whose difference in thought or religion threatened the Church.

Yet the significance of the Counter-Reformation went far beyond religious military conflicts, as the Counter-Reformation can be thought of as the first historical movement instigated by ruling institutions to preserve their monopoly on knowledge. From the Counter-Reformation onward, the control of knowledge by the state—or lack thereof—has been a major preoccupation of governing authorities. It can be seen in states and historical circumstances ranging from Metternich's censorship in Austria early in the nineteenth century to czarist Russia as well as their Soviet successors, the Nazis in Germany, and the authoritarian regimes in contemporary China and Russia.

It would be unimaginable to Martin Luther that his Renaissance pamphleteering has evolved into the singular global governance issue of the first quarter of the twenty-first century: what is fake news, what is real news, and who controls the information. Today's analogues to pamphleteering—electronic communication media like social media with unlimited scalability—can be both liberating and threatening to leadership in democracies and autocracies alike. And as the 2016 presidential election in the United States showed, it can also be used to disrupt the political culture of an adversary.

While the control of knowledge by authoritarian states has in principle become more essential, it has also weakened authoritarian states in the current age of human capital, hindering their ability to generate economic growth through technological creativity.

But what was true during Luther's time and during the Counter-Reformation against Lutheranism is true today: technological advancement and globalization are not the same, and correlation does not imply causation. Globalization and technology can play off each other and both may be culturally disruptive, but they are two decidedly distinct phenomena. As the printing press was disrupting the social order of Europe, globalization, in an earlier form known as the Age of Exploration, was simultaneously sweeping through Europe. Whether it was the tomato example in chapter 1, or the introduction of tobacco, sugar, and coffee or spices from the Far East, globalization was changing Renaissance Europe. Globalization at that time also had an amazing economic impact, first making Spain exceedingly rich, and then producing severe inflationary problems caused by the increased flow of silver and gold from South America. Yet the changes resulting from the Age of Exploration were not the same as those caused by the printing press. In fact, the Counter-Reformation did not attack globalization. The Catholic leadership saw the globalization of that time both as a holy mission to expand the true faith and as a way of gaining wealth.

Martin Luther's pamphlets attacking and calling for reforms in the sixteenth-century power structure ignited the conservative Counter-Reformation to protect the existing order of the time. In contrast, in the early twenty-first-century United States, it is the most conservative forces in American society, as well as ideological allies from abroad (discussed in greater depth in the following chapter), that are using the modern equivalents of the pamphlet to generate levels of fear in American society against globalization and the resulting changes. Social media and the internet have become the weapons of choice in the counterrevolution against globalization, with the misleading intertwining of globalization and technology.

In America, where technology and innovation are celebrated, it is difficult for people who benefit from the status quo to politically attack technology for creating economic and social disruption. Instead, a situation almost analogous to Freudian "displacement" occurs. *Displacement* is a psychological term that refers to an unconscious defense mechanism whereby the mind substitutes either a new aim or a new object for goals felt in their original form to be dangerous or unacceptable. So, in the United States during the first quarter of the twenty-first century, it was politically far easier to blame globalization and outsiders than technology for the economic commotion sweeping through areas of America.

From the earliest days of the republic, Americans have seen themselves as the inventive nation, the nation of change, and—whether correct or not—the singular home of technological innovation. Even the idea of creating a constitutional republic that put checks on government was both innovative and radical in an era dominated by hereditary monarchies and "enlightened absolutism." American culture reveled in technological and scientific innovation from its beginning. Whether Benjamin Franklin with electricity, Whitney with his cotton gin, Remington and his rifles, Alexander Graham Bell, Thomas Edison, or Henry Ford with the assembly line, the triumphs of these American innovators are deeply ingrained in the national culture and are part of every American middle and high school curriculum.

Culture represents both beliefs within a society and the patterns of custom that shape it. In this respect, American culture is particularly attuned to the development of innovation and technology. This cultural focus on innovation has also been a factor in why America has not seen strong antitechnology and antimachinery movements such as those that have taken place in Europe.

In England, the now-famous term *Luddites* emerged to describe followers of an antimachinery movement in the early part of the nine-teenth century. Named after Ned Ludd, the founder of the movement, the Luddites were a group of English textile workers who destroyed weaving machinery as a protest against the use of machinery as a way of getting around traditional labor standards. From their origin in Nottingham in 1811, Luddite movements spread rapidly through-out newly industrialized Britain, causing major economic disrup-tions during the height of the Napoleonic Wars. At one point, the British army had more men trying to suppress Luddite rebellions than they had fighting Napoleon in Spain. Finally, in 1812, the British Parliament passed the Frame Breaking Act, which made machine breaking a capital crime. Although the Luddite rebellion was put down by the British army in 1816, the word *Luddite* lives on, being applied today to anyone who opposes new technology.

About the same time as the Luddites, a similar movement whose name would likewise resonate throughout history was emerging in France. The word *sabotage* first came into popular use not as a way to describe a destructive action to hinder an enemy but as a word used by French workers to protest mechanical innovation. In the textile city of Lyon the workers threw their "sabots," or clogs, into textile machines as a means of destroying them. Because of their actions, the word *sabotage* evolved over time into meaning the delib-erate destruction of enemy property.

Luddite-type movements never gained wide support in the United States for three main reasons. Of course, first, America's culture emphasizes innovation and technological advancement. Second, since the country was established without a formal class system, antagonism in the early United States between those who had money and those who did not was less than that in Europe's aristocracy-dominated political systems. And third, the American industrial revolution began later, and consequently there was no overall loss of factory jobs caused by new machinery. In fact, the opposite was true, as booming American industrial capacity led to increased demand for factory workers, regardless of mechanical advances.

Perception though is always more important in politics than reality, and the outsider is easier to blame than oneself—or one's voters. A perception based on yesterday and fear of change is particularly easy to exploit. So the perception reinforced by antiglobalist rhetoric in the United States is that America in the first quarter of the twenty-first century is still bleeding manufacturing jobs—especially to China—and is increasingly drowning in illegal immigrants who are "stealing American jobs." Of course, this argument fails for the reason that in 2018 the United States had full employment. And according to a December 2018 study by the U.S. Department of Homeland Security (strangely, however, although the study was published by the government in 2018, the latest figures they have date to 2015) the unauthorized immigrant population in the United States stood at an estimated twelve million people, unchanged since 2009 and slightly down from a peak of 12.2 million in 2007.

Without a doubt, China's entry into the globalized world did absorb hundreds of thousands of American jobs, but this drain is no longer happening. Yet even with this large movement of manufacturing from the United States to China, the actual numbers are far less than the perception held by much of the American public.

According to the St. Louis Federal Reserve Bank in their report, "What Is the Impact of Chinese Imports on U.S. Jobs?," published on May 15, 2017,

> Of the more than 3 million manufacturing jobs that were lost overall in the U.S. between 2000 and 2007, we found that about 800,000 manufacturing jobs were lost because of the increased Chinese competition. Most of these jobs were in the production of computer and electronic goods, primary and fabricated metal products, furniture and textiles.
>
> As might be expected, larger states experienced larger losses in manufacturing jobs. After controlling for size, we found that states with a larger share of manufacturing employment (e.g., Ohio) experienced a larger than average loss, while the opposite was true for states with a smaller share of manufacturing employment (e.g., Florida).
>
> Despite the job losses in manufacturing, the economy gained a similar number of jobs in other sectors, such as services, con-

struction, and wholesale and retail trade. These sectors, which were not very exposed to Chinese competition, benefited from having access to cheaper intermediate inputs. As a result, U.S. firms in these sectors were able to lower their production costs. In turn, consumers were able to purchase these U.S. goods at a lower price. Between these savings and the savings on cheaper Chinese-made goods that they bought, U.S. consumers gained an average of $260 of extra spending per year for the rest of their lives, we estimated, all stemming from the increased imports from China.

Beginning around 2005, manufacturing jobs stopped moving en masse from the United States to China for several reasons. First, the massive Chinese industrial growth during the period 1980–2000 had, for the most part, already absorbed most large-scale labor-intensive manufacturing, such as garments, shoes, and general-assembly-based jobs. Second, labor costs in China were rising significantly. Third, integrated-supply-chain manufacturing became more cost-effective. Fourth, and very important, fracking technology emerged, thus enabling the United States to have the cheapest natural gas among any of its industrial competitors. Finally, there was an increase in automation and the development of artificial intelligence.

While at the same time American companies began to rethink the economic benefits of offshoring service jobs, that is, sending jobs to cheaper offshore labor markets. Back in 2006 Alan Blinder of Princeton University, looking at the trend at that time, wrote about how offshoring could devastate the U.S. service industry and take away many nonindustrial jobs. In fact he forecasted that a quarter or more of U.S. service-based jobs would be vulnerable to this trend.

What appears to have happened, however, is that offshoring of service jobs became in many cases economically inefficient. Blinder recognized how time and business practicality proved much of his forecast to be incorrect. He was quoted in a *New York Times* piece by Ben Casselman on September 27, 2019: "Where in retrospect I missed the boat is in thinking that the gigantic gap in labor costs between here and India would push it to India rather than to South

Dakota." Blinder then said, "There were other aspects of the costs to moving the activities that we weren't thinking about very much back then when people were worrying about offshoring."

In essence what had happened between 2006 and 2019 is that American business found that the labor savings of offshoring of service jobs were offset by other factors: time differences, language barriers, legal hurdles, and the simple challenge of coordinating work half a world away. Also offshoring doesn't work when one needs to understand the specifics of business or have knowledge of the customer.

So what happened is that companies decided they were better off moving jobs to less expensive parts of the United States rather than offshoring. A prime example of this point is happening as I write this paragraph: JPMorgan Chase is considering moving a substantial part of its workforce out of midtown Manhattan to Texas.

But the real disrupter—not to the national unemployment numbers per se but to a feeling of dislocation and economic uncertainty—has been automation. As Dani Rodrick of the Kennedy School of Government at Harvard University points out, "By all accounts, automation and new digital technologies played a quantitatively greater role in deindustrialization and in spatial and income inequalities. But globalization became tainted with a stigma of unfairness that technology evaded."

While the Metropolitan Policy Program of the Brookings Institute stated,

> Many believe that the loss of manufacturing jobs over the last few decades is a result of American companies "offshoring" their manufacturing plants and/or due to American consumers buying more foreign manufactured goods. These people often propose protectionist trade measures (like tariffs) in order to revive manufacturing employment.
>
> However, most economists agree that the decline in manufacturing employment is a result of increasing productivity, not foreign competition.

Economists from Ball State University report that, "Had we kept 2000-levels of productivity and applied them to 2010-levels of production we would have required 20.9 million manufacturing workers. Instead, we employed only 12.1 million." They estimate that nearly 90% of the manufacturing job losses are attributable to productivity growth. Though some other economists, like David Autor, have found this percentage to be around 75%. Just as employment shifted from agriculture to manufacturing 100 years ago due to productivity gains, now employment is shifting from manufacturing to the service and knowledge sectors.

Protectionist measures will do little to revive manufacturing employment, but they likely will harm hundreds of millions of American consumers as well as the domestic businesses who use imported intermediate and capital goods in their production processes. The costs probably outweigh the benefits. Consider that, when asked by the University of Chicago if raising import tariffs on products like cars was a good idea, not a single economist agreed. Also, ". . . in 2011, government tariffs imposed on Chinese tire imports to protect US industry likely saved some 1,200 jobs. At the same time, the total cost to American consumers from higher tire prices was roughly $1 billion in 2011 and the cost per job saved at least $900,000 that year."

In fact, the 2016 Global Manufacturing Competitiveness Index report from Deloitte Global and the Council on Competitiveness reported that the United States is expected to take over the number one manufacturing position from China by 2020. The report goes on to say that the U.S. continued to improve its ranking from fourth in 2010 to third in 2013 to second in the 2016 study. Moreover, executives expected the U.S. to assume the top position before the end of the decade.

To understand why the American position has climbed so rapidly, one need only look to hydraulic fracking as evidence. The United States is now the world's largest producer of natural gas, which is crucial in competitive heavy industrial manufacturing. Due to domestic production increases, it is now substantially cheaper to purchase natural gas in America than in Europe or Asia. American gas sold at the end of 2017 for about $3.72 per million BTU, compared with about $4.98 in Europe and $7.30 in Asia. According to the International Monetary Fund, this advantage has led to a 6 percent increase, on average, in America's manufactured exports because of greater competitiveness.

The International Energy Agency has warned that Europe will lose a third of its share of global-energy-intensive exports over the next two decades, because its energy prices will remain higher than those in the U.S. The agency did not mention China, but obviously the situation should be similar to Europe in reference to non-labor-intensive and non-energy-intensive manufacturing.

By the way, the benefits to the U.S. economy from fracking—setting aside, if one can, the environmental negatives—bring us back to the comment I made in chapter 4 in reference to Americans liking to talk like Jefferson in reference to limited government and industry but to act like Hamilton. Since the 1970s the U.S. government has spent over $100 million funding basic research into fracking, while extending tax breaks to companies involved in the industry. As Dan Steward, an executive at Mitchel Energy, where fracking was first successfully developed, stated, "[The U.S. Department of Energy] did a hell of a lot of work, and I can't give them enough credit for that. DOE started it, and other people took the ball and ran with it. You cannot diminish the DOE's involvement."

Unfortunately, the renewed growth of manufacturing in the United States does not mean a massive return of high-paying manufacturing jobs. It does not mean the revitalization of the former American midwestern industrial cities on account of these jobs or the alleviation of the frustration of the middle-aged factory worker who perceives his or her worth in the society is declining daily; quite the opposite.

This paradox leads directly to the biggest misrepresentation of the antiglobalists, and in some respects the biggest mystery. These jobs are not coming back simply because they no longer exist. The high-paying industrial jobs that comprised a major part of the postwar American workforce are no longer central to the economic growth of a modern knowledge-based economy. They are similar to the work the medieval monks did in Europe, handwriting books before Gutenberg's invention of the printing press. The tariff increases and trade renegotiations demanded by the antiglobalists will not change this situation. So the question then becomes, what is the reason for the antiglobalist leadership to spur on a counterfactual movement? This is the crux of the political problem, which in principle has nothing to do with globalization. Economic culture has changed from the age of manufacturing to the age of human capital.

If anything, in reality the manufacturing situation will probably actually get worse, at least in terms of total employment numbers. A 2017 study by McKinsey and Company concluded that by 2030, 39 million to 73 million American jobs could be replaced by automation and advances in artificial intelligence. While the report estimates that 20 million people could be moved into similar occupations doing slightly different tasks, that still means 16 million to 54 million people—or about one-third of the U.S. workforce—will need to be retrained for totally new occupations.

Susan Lund, McKinsey's director of research and a coauthor of the study said,

> The biggest problem will be retraining millions of workers mid-career. Governments and businesses already have fallen short in the retraining of workers who lost jobs in the recession of 2007 to 2009.
>
> The big question isn't, "Will there be jobs?" The big question is, "Will people who lost jobs be able to get new ones?"

What is fascinating about our current period in America—with technology disrupting cultural norms and the blame being laid on perceived others—is that it is a recurring theme in American history. In chapter 4, I wrote about how the rise of the automobile in the 1920s helped disrupt American farm economics, leading to calls for higher tariffs. Setting aside the fact that today agricultural pricing is not a major concern, the second decade of the twenty-first century in American society mirrors very closely the 1920s in how the political culture dealt with massive technological changes of the time.

The 1920s were the high point of that time for the technological, innovative, and consumer changes that derived from the industrial revolution. From the 1920s until the advent of the children of Gordon Moore's musings on computer speeds, the predominant technological innovations introduced were essentially upgrades and improvements to techniques first introduced in the 1920s. Just look at the commercial airline industry, where the first regularly scheduled flight occurred on May 23, 1926, between Salt Lake City and Los Angeles. Airliners transformed from propeller planes to jet aircraft, and from planes holding ten to fifteen people to those carrying more than five hundred, but the underlying concepts did not change. The same thing could be said for the automobile, as well as the multitude of electronic products that came into mass-market use in the 1920s, whether refrigerators, washing machines, or radios.

Like today, the 1920s in America were a time of spectacular wealth and an ever-increasing income gap. And just like America in the second decade of the twenty-first century, it was a period of unprecedented highs in the stock market.

The 1920s shared yet another characteristic with our current period: that of great migration within the country. Cities became the rage. The 1920 census showed that for the first time, more Americans lived in cities than in the countryside. In that census, 51 percent of Americans lived in urban areas. By the 1930 census, that number had risen to 56 percent.

Like the decline of small rural cities that is happening in America today, the great rural heartland in the 1920s went through massive technological changes that led to a huge migration to the cities. As American farms became increasingly mechanized, there was simply no need for nearly half of the traditional agricultural jobs. In 1890 the U.S. Department of Agriculture reported that it took forty to fifty hours of labor to produce one hundred bushels of wheat on five acres with a gang plow, seeder, harrow, binder, thresher, wagons, and horses. By 1930 it took fifteen to twenty hours of labor to produce one hundred bushels of wheat on five acres with a three-bottom gang plow, tractor, ten-foot tandem disk, harrow, twelve-foot combine, and trucks.

This change was accelerated by a rapid decline in the cost of farm machinery, similar to the decline in the cost of computing power today. A farm tractor in 1920 cost about $785. Just two years later, the price had dropped to $395, making the tractor an affordable piece of equipment for almost every farmer.

Ironically, when new technology is introduced, the full economic benefit of that technology often takes time to work its way through the logjam of human tradition and culture. Technology that might be viewed as revolutionary often falls into the usage patterns of the device it was replacing. Such was the case with the farm tractor. It arrived at whirlwind speeds on the farm in the 1920s, but some of the more important benefits of the tractor to farm economics would take decades to emerge. Although in the 1920s the tractor mostly replaced the horse, farming methods continued to adhere to patterns established for horse-driven plowing for several more decades. A possible analogue today is the continued strength of printed book sales, despite the advent of the e-reader.

The best example of this related to the tractor is in the arcane but important agricultural subject of row width, the unplanted area between rows of corn and other grains. Until the late 1940s and even as late as the early 1950s, the width between rows of corn was forty to forty-four inches. This measurement was based on the size of a horse's rump, that is, how wide the row needs to be to let the horse pass through it. Eventually, people realized with tractors and various new farm equipment this requirement was no longer necessary, and row width between lines of crops became significantly smaller. Currently, row widths range from fifteen to thirty-eight inches. The advantage of the narrower row width is enormous, as farmers can use the same planting equipment for corn and soybeans, and the narrower width reduces weed competition, increases shading of the soil, and increases light interception per plant. All of these factors have greatly increased yield and improved the economics of farming.

The roaring twenties were an urban dream for the millennials of that time who could adapt. The flappers, the speakeasies, the jazz, and early Hollywood were no different from contemporary Brooklyn or Silicon Valley. In the middle of the country, however, the situation was also similar to the current era, with the economy at best languishing and at worst outright depressed. In a remarkably short time, a very noticeable cultural and economic divide developed between the urban and rural classes.

Many social historians see the 1920s as a beginning of the slow move toward women's liberation in America. First and foremost was the ratification of the Nineteenth Amendment to the U.S. Constitution on August 18, 1920, which granted American women the right to vote. But there was also the urban cultural flapper revolution of short dresses, short hairstyles, and a new sense of freedom. Technologically, there were the liberating devices of the refrigerator, washing machine, vacuum cleaner, and electric iron. At the same time, the word *coed*—at the time a liberating term—moved into common usage. Today, one questions why there was a need for such a word in the first place.

Except for the right to vote, the majority of these extraordinary changes—both cultural and technological—never extended beyond urban America. Most women in rural America could not easily adapt the latest flapper fashions or enjoy what appeared to be the cornucopia of the new Jazz Age. They were making their own clothes that they washed by hand and were growing their own food, which they needed to preserve with ice since much of rural America was not yet electrified. Compounding this disparity between the urban and the rural was the reality that as farming became more mechanized, the demand for rural labor dropped faster than people were able or willing to move off the farm. Trapped in an area of rapidly declining employment opportunities and trying to keep their families together, most rural women found that basic subsistence was a higher priority. Just as today, although the lights of the city might have been very bright, it was difficult to move and to adapt to a new, frightening culture.

The rapid technological change of the 1920s, the inability of a large minority of people to adapt to changes, and the inability of political leadership to explain and guide the change caused a break in the traditional American political equilibrium.

And here the political parallels between 1920s America and the first quarter of the twenty-first century in America become striking, especially if one looks at the advent of a political "counterreformation" against the changes technology was making on the culture. While leaders of this movement in the 1920s did not have job loss to Asia as a whipping boy, they were nonetheless using globalization as a scapegoat and responding to an electorate overwhelmed by change. Political displacement was in full bloom, and it was much easier to blame the outsider than to blame the technological innovation of the time, whether automobiles, tractors, or the economic and cultural appeal of the city.

The word *globalization* had not yet been coined in the 1920s; in fact, it first came into general usage when the Harvard economist Theodore Levitt wrote an article titled "Globalization of Markets" for the *Harvard Business Review* in 1983. But irrespective of the words used, the concept it implied was understood. In the 1920s, the antonym of globalization—isolationism—became the key political term of the period. Isolationism was a diplomatic and economic doctrine that aimed to make the United States economically self-reliant, separate from the evils of the outside world. It attempted to isolate the United States from the diplomatic affairs of other countries by avoiding foreign entanglements and alliances. As someone in the Office of the Historian of the U.S. Department of State wrote, "During the 1920s, the United States strongly resisted binding international commitments." The political emphasis on isolationism, sovereignty, and autonomy are strikingly similar to the ideological underpinnings of the Trump administration, as evidenced by its denuding of the State Department, its rejection of the Trans-Pacific Partnership treaty and the Paris Agreement on climate change.

Like the antiglobalist philosophy of our current period, the isolationism of the 1920s meant keeping America separate from "others," whether immigrants or products. Donald Trump's anti-immigrant rhetoric is a replay of the harsh anti-immigrant language of the 1920s. Republican congressman Albert Johnson of Washington state, a leader of the anti-immigrant movement in the 1920s, was quoted in the *Literary Digest*, the leading weekly magazine of the time: "We are being made a dumping ground. We are receiving the dependents, the human wreckage of the war; not the strength and virility that once came to hew our forests and till our soil. And worst of all, they are coming in such numbers when we are unable adequately to take care of them."

In 1921, *Good Housekeeping* ran an article by Vice President Coolidge titled "Whose Country Is This?," in which he stated, "There can't be too many inhabitants of the right kind, the vicious, the weak of body, the shiftless, or the improvident," the "suicidal . . . inflowing of cheap manhood, constitutes a danger in our midst. Some immigrants, politically twisted agitators, came with a set desire to teach destruction of government. Others may not have been intent on treachery, but there were still racial considerations too grave to be brushed aside."

And in support of halting immigration from southern and eastern Europe, Coolidge went on: "While Nordics propagate themselves successfully, race mixing shows deterioration on both sides." The anti-immigration firestorm of the 1920s also parallels contemporary American political culture in that it was partly based on the fear of loss of power, status, and influence by the Anglo-Saxon political majority. When translated into political terms, these fears became explicitly racial.

The anti-immigration fever led to the passage of the Immigration Act of 1924. According to the U.S. Department of State Office of the Historian, the fundamental purpose of the law was "to preserve the ideal of American homogeneity."

The law based national immigration quotas into the United States on a population baseline from the 1890 census, thus drastically limiting Asian and European immigrants perceived as radical and "un-American": Italians, Poles, eastern Europeans, and Jews. Before the enactment of this law, millions of immigrants came into the United States. By 1929 only 150,000 immigrants per year were allowed in.

As the American Anthropological Association wrote in a piece describing that time as part of their Race in the USA timeline series on May 27, 2008:

> Discriminatory immigration policies aimed at southern and eastern Europeans figured into the quota-based policies of the 1920s. With the passage of the Immigration Act of 1924, also known as the National Origins Act or Johnson-Reed Act, the U.S. used restrictive immigration policies in the 1920s based on the 1890 proportions of foreign-born European nationalities. Since the 1890 census reflected higher numbers of northern Europeans, immigrants from those countries had greater opportunities to emigrate. The arguments, outlined in Madison Grant's 1916 book *The Passing of a Great Race*, held that older immigrants were skilled, thrifty, hardworking like native-born Americans and recent immigrants from southern and eastern Europe were unskilled, ignorant, predominantly Catholic or Jewish and not easily assimilated into American culture. Madison Grant and Charles Davenport, among other eugenicists, were called in as expert advisers on the threat of "inferior stock" from eastern and southern Europe, playing a critical role as Congress debated the Immigration Act of 1924. The act attempted to control the number of "unfit" individuals entering the country by lowering the number of immigrants allowed in to fifteen percent of what it had been previously. Existing laws prohibiting race mixing were strengthened as well. The adoption of incest laws and many anti-miscegenation laws were also influenced by the premises of eugenics.

And as Senator Reed of Pennsylvania—one of the main architects of the immigration act—argued on the Senate floor, "Earlier legislation disregards entirely those of us who are interested in keeping American stock up to the highest standard—that is, the people who were born here."

Isolationism meant separation not just from people but also from products. In 1922 Congress passed the Fordney-McCumber Act: essentially a dress rehearsal for the Smoot-Hawley Act. The Fordney-McCumber Act introduced the highest tariffs in American history up to that time. The law raised the American tariff rate to an average of about 38.5 percent for dutiable imports, and an average of 14 percent overall.

Like Smoot-Hawley to come, the Fordney-McCumber Act was passed to pacify the agricultural base of the Republican Party. During World War I, American farmers economically boomed, as they needed to supply not only the United States but also war-torn Europe with food. Not seeing this as just a short-term turn of luck, American farmers borrowed heavily to expand their output. By 1922, with the war over for four years, Europe no longer needed huge quantities of American agriculture, and prices for agricultural commodities in the United States collapsed. Instead of enjoying continued prosperity, farmers were now unable to repay the bank loans they had taken out to expand production.

Like Smoot-Hawley, the Fordney-McCumber Act was a false political response to a problem, blaming America's trading partners for an economic condition that had nothing to do with trade. The tragedy that befell American agriculture due to overplanting and the farmers' naive belief that Europe would need the same amount of product in peacetime as it did in war had nothing to do with trade or with the negligible amounts of food being exported from Europe to the United States. The Fordney-McCumber Act of 1922 was a purely political salve that in its application ended up making life on the farm more difficult, as well as intensifying the growing debt crisis over the repayment of war loans to United States financial institutions.

Not surprising is that America's trading partners immediately responded to Fordney-McCumber by raising their own tariffs. Amazingly, the likelihood of retaliatory tariffs being implemented was a lesson somehow forgotten eight years later during the Smoot-Hawley debate. It is also a lesson that is being ignored as this chapter is being written. Raising tariffs is not like raising in a round of friendly poker. In poker a player can choose not to raise and drop out of the hand without any embarrassment. When a country raises tariffs, its trading partner or rival can't drop out of the game without appearing weak to its constituents at home; consequently, the public pressure to retaliate becomes acute. So, whether rightfully or not, the trading partner bids up the game, raising their tariffs and escalating the potential for economic crisis. Thus, immediately after Fordney-McCumber was enacted, Spain raised its tariffs on American goods by 40 percent, and Germany and Italy significantly raised their tariffs on American wheat.

The fact that Europeans raised their tariffs on American agriculture was again a restatement of the old saying, "Be careful what you wish for." Even with their isolation-focused mindset, the inability of the U.S. Congress to appreciate that their actions might have reactions, and that raising tariffs would likely cause a retaliation, is staggering. As with Smoot-Hawley to come, in 1922 substantially more American agriculture products were sold to Europe than the Europeans were selling to America. Consequently, the protectionist medication prescribed to the farmers by Congress actually made their situation far worse than it had been.

The Fordney-McCumber Act also hurt farmers and the American economy as a whole in another way. The act had a particularly onerous provision on tariff calculation known as "the American Selling Price." The best way to explain the effects of the American Selling Price calculation is to quote the example Senator William E. Borah of Idaho gave seven years after the tariff was passed in discussing its failures:

> For example, if a set amount of a foreign-produced chemical had a value in its home market of $60 and the U.S. tariff rate for that item was 50 percent, then the total price on the American market would be $90 ($60 + $30—a common way of calculation tariffs). However, that item might be in short supply in the U.S. and could command a market price of $80. Under Fordney-McCumber, the statutory 50 percent rate would be applied to the higher American selling price and result in an overall price of $120 ($80 + 40). The rate remained unchanged, but it would be harder for foreign producers to market their product in the U.S.

The American Selling Price provision had one major effect at that time: inflation. It allowed domestic manufacturers—now basically free from foreign competition—to raise their prices. Setting aside the extremely aggressive manner in which the American Selling Price provision allowed tariffs to be calculated, it demonstrates one of the basic problems when mature, developed countries set high tariff walls, whether in 1922 or 2018: the rise in domestic prices.

The American Selling Price provision was a sucker punch to the American farmer of the 1920s. By raising the tariff on various industrial parts that were needed in farm equipment and in fact making it uneconomical to import these parts at all, prices on farm equipment rose substantially. According to Edward S. Kaplan of the City University in New York writing about the effects on the tariff for the Economic History Association, the average harness set that sold for $46 in 1918 sold for $75 in 1926. At the same time the fourteen-inch plow doubled in cost from $14 to $28, mowing machines went from $45 to $95, and farm wagons increased in price from $85 to $150.

Besides not helping the American farmer, the Fordney-McCumber Act of 1922 presents a powerful lesson about the naivete of isolationism. While the 1922 world was not globalized as we know it today and although isolationism was the fashion of the time, the financial industry, as we have seen in chapter 1 with the loans of the Dutch bankers to America's Continental Congress, had already been globalized for centuries. During World War I, the United States lent various European nations $7 billion, and lent an additional $3.3 billion after the war for reconstruction and recovery. However, with much of its economy devastated by the war, Europe could not meet its debt obligations to the United States. Compounding this problem was that Europe had shipped most of its gold to the United States during the war to pay for American goods.

With European markets in shambles, the easiest way European countries could earn money to pay off these huge debts was by exporting products to the United States. But with the Fordney-McCumber Act of 1922 substantially raising the duty on European products, it made implementation of that concept much more difficult. As Sir Josiah Stamp, a British banker and industrialist, stated, "Debt payments could not be made unless the Fordney-McCumber

Tariff was reduced to enable the European nations to sell their goods in the United States."

To help alleviate the debt problem, in 1924 the Coolidge administration initiated the Dawes Plan, which was a loan of $200 million in gold so that Germany could revive its economy and pay its reparations to the allied nations, who could, in turn, repay their debts to U.S. banks. Ironically, the Dawes Plan was a 1924 version of globalized finance initiated by the isolationist Coolidge regime. Yet the reality is that this convoluted scheme probably would not have been necessary in the first place if there had not been the Fordney-McCumber Act.

When it comes to the problem of international debt repayment, the Fordney-McCumber Act is a lesson in how judicious any major country must be in raising tariffs, even though it was enacted in the 1920s and the United States had not yet seized the crown of global hegemony. Like the Smoot-Hawley Act to come, the Fordney-McCumber Act demonstrated the inherent problem American leadership has in balancing the interests of a domestic constituency against the broader interest of both the country and the world. No one can blame an American political leader for trying to pacify his or her base, but when it is done though the bludgeon of tariffs without taking into account international repercussions, much more is lost than gained.

Tariffs are often the nationalist economic version of censorship. In their most detrimental form, they destroy the concept of competitiveness that is the underlining hallmark of the capitalist system. As a hypothetical example, why would Apple work twenty-four seven to make a better cell phone if they knew Samsung would be prevented from entering the American market due to high tariffs or through tariff calculations like the American Selling Price system? More often than not, tariffs represent the false economic promise of the antiglobalist. Tariffs are like a sugar high that a child will get from eating too much birthday cake. The child will feel wonderful and silly at first but then drained and very cranky.

In advanced economies, tariffs are also often gifts to the status quo, to the old industries facing technological or global competitive pressure. Economists label this gift "rent-seeking," which is defined as a company or organization obtaining an economic gain—usually through political relations—without giving back any benefits to society. In the case of tariffs, a domestic company gets to raise its prices, since the cheaper foreign competition is now out of the market, but they do not need to do anything to improve their product to justify the price increase.

Obviously, history could not directly predict the future, especially between now and the 1920s when there had been so much intervening history setting various paths for human behavior. But that does not mean history is not a lesson, and its failures and success should be learned like a child learns that she will get hurt when she touches a hot stove. The 1920s were a period of American history when isolationism—not globalization—dominated, when the fear of the other was transcendent and technology and innovation were running wild through the economy, radically disrupting traditional patterns of life. It was a period of booming prosperity mixed with radical change.

In terms of globalization, three major points separate the first quarter of the twentieth century in America from the first quarter of the twenty-first century. First, we are now living in an age of globalization with the United States as the hegemon. To pretend that we could isolate ourselves is pure sophistry. Second, unlike the 1920s, massive factories are not being built and employing hundreds of thousands of people in the United States—in fact, just the opposite. And third, Moore's Law has taken over. The exponential growth in the speed of change and the inability of many humans to adjust to constant change both create fear and challenge the basic concept of plodding representative democracy.

The 1920s, a lush decade that ended in disaster, are the perfect example of why the counterreformation against globalization is ultimately a counterrevolution against tomorrow. In the next and final chapter we look at what must be done both nationally and internationally to insure that the fear of change, a phrase that has become politically synonymous with globalization, does not destroy our democracy, and at how globalization makes the United States not only safer but more powerful.

SEVEN

Tomorrow

G lobalization is so much more than the definitions I gave in the introduction. It is the human economic and cultural version of evolution. It is a natural phenomenon pushing humans into more efficient behavior that combines the rationale of the market with the human need to explore, change, and grow. It moves cultures and societies forward as one new idea challenges or blends into another.

Just as biological evolution moves in fits and starts, goes off on tangents, and then moves forward, so does globalization. A key difference, however, is that as far as we know, biological evolution cannot be felt individually by humans, since it takes place over thousands of years. In contrast, globalization is felt immediately; not only is it felt, but it can also cause pain and almost immediately create winners and losers. Except for the occasional appendectomy, few people care that they carry around in their body an appendix, a blind-ended tube somewhat connected to the colon that scientist speculate our ancient ancestors needed to help digest foliage. But many people do care when they can no longer adapt economically, or when their traditional culture, which has supported their values for generations, becomes threatened by new concepts and what appear to be foreign patterns of behavior. Societies have been globalizing since before the beginning of human record, when a new tribe was conquered or chose to adapt the more efficient ways of another tribe. There have always been people who could not adapt, who felt threatened and could not flourish under the new ways. And there were always people who of course benefited from the old system and would lose their position—whether status or wealth—under globalized change.

Here is where fundamental economic laws dating back to Adam Smith, the so-called father of modern economics, play a significant role. Smith wrote about how wealth was created, and one of his prime tenets in the creation of wealth was sharing skills, specialization, and open markets. As Steven Pinker, in his wonderful book *Enlightenment Now: The Case for Reason, Science, Humanism, and Progress*, described it,

> [Adam] Smith noted that an abundance of useful stuff cannot be conjured into existence by a farmer or craftsman working in isolation. It depends on a network of specialists, each of whom learns how to make something as efficiently as possible, and who combine and exchange the fruits of their ingenuity, skill, and labor.
>
> In a famous example, Smith calculated that a pin-maker working alone could make at most one pin a day, whereas in a workshop in which "one man draws out the wire, another straights it, a third cuts it, a fourth points it, a fifth grinds it at the top for receiving the head," each could make almost five thousand.
>
> Specialization works only in a market that allows the specialists to exchange their goods and services, and Smith explained that economic activity was a form of mutually beneficial cooperation (a positive-sum game, in today's lingo): each gets back something that is more valuable to him than what he gives up. Through voluntary exchange, people benefit others by benefiting themselves; as he wrote, "It is not from the benevolence of the butcher, the brewer, or the baker that we expect our dinner, but from their regard to their own interest. We address ourselves, not to their humanity but to their self-love." Smith was not saying that people are ruthlessly selfish, or that they ought to be; he was one of history's keenest commentators on human sympathy. He only said that in a market, whatever tendency people have to care for their families and themselves can work to

the good of all. Exchange can make an entire society not just richer but nicer, because in an effective market it is cheaper to buy things than to steal them, and other people are more valuable to you alive than dead.

Repeatedly through the centuries, societies that have tried to prevent globalization have withered, ultimately failing in their attempt to stop the exchange of goods, ideas, and people. And the word *people* here is key: immigration to many, especially in Western countries, represents the most threatening and fearful part of globalization. Anti-immigration is the "Sieg Heil" of the antiglobalization movement. Anti-immigration, not economic dislocation, is the common denominator, the rallying cry of the forces most opposed to globalization. There are few better examples than when Donald Trump announced his candidacy for the presidency and included the following words: "When Mexico sends its people, they're not sending their best. They're not sending you. They're not sending you. They're sending people that have lots of problems, and they're bringing those problems with us. They're bringing drugs. They're bringing crime. They're rapists."

Yet if one looks at the history of immigration, the United States is a wonderful example of how new cultures, new ideas, and—often out of necessity—a more aggressive work ethic can dramatically stimulate the local economy.

Kellogg Insights, the online research journal of the Kellogg School of Management at Northwestern University, conducted a fascinating study with the title "Does Immigration Help or Hurt Local Economies?," followed by the tagline "Historically, where immigrants cluster in the U.S., prosperity follows." The researchers looked at historic patterns of immigration into the United States. In particular, they thought the best way to see how immigration would affect the country economically in the future was to look at the effects it had previously, especially looking at the age of mass immigration into the United States between 1860 and 1920.

Their main research question was "In the long run, did areas with more immigration end up better off?" They found without a doubt, yes. Their study shows that counties that were the center of immigration a century ago today "have much higher incomes, less poverty, and lower unemployment, among other perks." Amazingly, the research also demonstrated that "if a county that experienced no immigration during this period (1860–1920) had instead experienced median levels of immigration, residents today would have a 20 percent higher per capita income."

Another interesting factor of this study that leads directly to the economic benefits of globalization is the role of railroads in the nineteenth century and the early part of the twentieth. I mentioned in the introduction how both the Austro-Hungarian emperor and the czar of Russia tried to limit railroad construction in the nineteenth century, out of fear that radical "foreign ideas" would spread in their empires. In the United States, railroad construction was supported by the federal government through land grants and was seen as a way of both uniting the vast country and stimulating the economy. But according to the Kellogg study, railroad growth in the United States had another function related to immigration, directly contradicting the fear of railroad growth espoused by the emperor and the czar.

In the United States the immigrants moved to their new homes, in general, on the expanding railroad network. Somewhat ironically, however, this function was partly determined by the ups and downs in the waves of immigration due to political turmoil, pogroms, and revolutions in eastern Europe and Russia, as well as the results of climatic changes such as the Irish potato famine.

Because of the randomness of these events, the study shows fascinatingly that during the period of railroad growth, U.S. counties that got connected to the railway right before a political or climatic shock in Europe would get many more immigrants than counties connected to the railroad after the traumatic events happened in Europe. The basic fact, however, remains true: immigration was a tremendous positive to economic development and the railroad system was not somehow a threat but the highway that enabled this catalyst of growth to occur.

In 2017 Moody's Analytics found that there is a direct correlation between increased immigration and a rise in America's gross domestic product (GDP). This correlation between immigration and GDP growth continues today. For every 1 percent increase in immigrants to the U.S., the country's GDP rises 1.25 percent. And in the fall of 2017 the National Academies of Sciences, Engineering, and Medicine released a report concluding that immigration to the United States from 1990 to 2010, both legal and illegal, produced net benefits worth $50 billion a year to the native population.

But if the economic argument for controlled and methodical immigration is logical (and by *controlled* I mean not a total opening of borders, because no country could exist as a governing organization if it was overwhelmed by an immediate massive influx of immigrants), why is the key rallying point against globalization a fear of immigration? Why is immigration the bogeyman that is constantly used to attack globalization? Just look at how Donald Trump continues to act politically; every time his polls drop or he seems to get into additional problems he attacks immigration and screams about building the wall. Trump is hardly the sole political leader to embrace xenophobia either; similar rhetoric about immigration comes out of the National Front in France, the Brexit supporters in the UK, and the current political leadership of Poland and Hungary.

First, of course, immigration is globalization head-on. It is not like going to the Indian restaurant in Wichita, Kansas, where the spices have been modified to fit American taste patterns. The immigrant community is the other, settling in what appears to be strange neighborhoods with similar immigrants, forming ghettos of the other. Second, it is easy to play on the fear of the other during periods of economic stress or change. And for some, immigration and job outsourcing are just opposite sides of the same coin: you lost your job to foreign competition and now those same foreigners are coming into your country to take your job.

It is interesting, however, that only in the United States are so-called unfair trade practices given almost equal weight to anti-immigration in the rhetorical mumbo jumbo of the antiglobalist. In Europe the antiglobalist rhetoric doesn't attack China for how its trade practices treat the European Union unfairly. There have been basically no rallying cries in Europe for massive trade wars against China or political comments about how China has taken advantage of the EU. In fact, in a position totally opposite the anti-globalist thinking in America, one of the arguments for Brexit (a major victory for the antiglobalist) was that in leaving the EU, the UK would be able to more freely take advantage of free trade and establish its own trade relationship with China.

Dani Rodrick, at Harvard's Kennedy School, suggests that anti-trade is not an effective argument in Europe because of Europe's vastly superior social welfare safety net. Rodrick states,

> One difference with the U.S. that may account for this contrast is that Europe has long had strong social protections and a generous welfare state. Most countries of Europe, being smaller than the U.S., are much more open to trade. But openness to trade has been accompanied by much greater redistribution and social insurance. A number of empirical analyses have shown that there is a direct link between exposure to trade and expansion of public transfers. . . . It is not an exaggeration to say that the European welfare state is the flip side of the open economy.

History is also a major factor in why the Europeans are not as threatened as Americans are by globalized change brought on by trade. As Rodrick stated, Europe is mainly smaller countries, and from the time of the formation of these countries and even before then, trade was key for survival. As an example, in the 1100s, long before many countries in northern Europe existed, the Hanseatic League, a medieval forerunner to the European Union, regulated and controlled the Baltic Sea trade for almost three centuries. Then there was Florence, a wool center in the Middle Ages that needed dyes from the Middle East to color the wool, and Venice, which on account of international trade grew into the extraordinarily wealthy and powerful Renaissance city-state that we know of. On the contrary, the United States up until the mid-1980s was generally a self-sufficient continental market. This is not to say that the United States did not trade or export; for sure it did, as we have just seen by the effects the tariffs of the 1920s had on the U.S. economy. Until recently, however, trade in the United States had been a much smaller part of the American economy than in Europe. In Europe, with various countries being literally across the street from another, international trade was a normal part of life for more than a millennium.

History alone fails, however, when it comes to understanding why the word *immigration* inflames antiglobalist rhetoric in both Europe and the United States. Obviously, the United States is a country of immigrants, from Donald Trump's wife and mother to the founding fathers of the country being mostly grandchildren or great-grandchildren of immigrants. In fact, everyone living in America, except for Native Americans and descendants of African slaves, can trace their American roots directly to a forebear immigrating. Europe of course is different in this regard.

If there is one thing that unites Europe, it is not immigration, at least for more than a millennium, but a common history of Christian culture, whether outwardly practiced or not. And throughout that common history, right or wrong, there has been one shared enemy: the infidel. At times this term referred to Jews, but more often—especially in terms of conquest and warfare—it referred to Muslims. It is a history of antagonism that goes back more than thirteen hundred years. In 732 the Frankish leader Charles Martel stopped the invading Spanish Moors, who were Muslim, from seizing France at the Battle of Tours. Then there were the Crusades by the Europeans to free the Holy Land from the Muslim infidels starting in 1095 and lasting for approximately two hundred years.

In 1492 the Spanish monarchs Ferdinand and Isabella defeated the last of the Muslim Moors in Spain. This so-called victory for Spain ironically was a major defeat for early globalization. Moorish Spain was one of the most cosmopolitan places in the world, with a standard of living greatly surpassing that of the Christian areas of the country.

The story of conflict between European Christianity and nearby Muslim nations continues into the seventeenth century. In 1683 a united European army defeated seventy thousand Ottomans at the gates of Vienna. An interesting related story: Before I became an academic I was the head of the North American trade division of a major Austrian bank. In my first trip to visit the bank, and my first trip to the wonderful city of Vienna, my managing director took me on a walking tour of Vienna. He pointed out a rusty circular metal object on the outside wall of an old building and asked me if I knew what that was. I said I had no idea. He pointed out that it was a cannonball from the Ottomans when they tried to take Vienna. Historical memory runs deep.

That memory also pertains to Austria's former imperial partner, Hungary. From approximately 1526 to 1687, the Ottomans occupied much of Hungary. To some extent, one can see how Viktor Orbán's fanatical anti-immigrant campaign for reelection as prime minister of Hungary in 2018 resonates within the Hungarian collective historic consciousness. The problem here is the role of the leader; in reality Hungary gains little in a globalized world by following someone who plays off historic fears instead of leading for tomorrow. But when leadership's concern is remaining in power, attacking the outsider, cosmopolitanism, and globalization is often a more effective tactic than a sober analysis of reality. As Mária Schmidt, a conservative Hungarian historian and supporter of Viktor Orbán, stated in an attack on what she sees as interference by the EU in Hungary's move to an illiberal democracy, "[EU leaders have] committed themselves to a utopian and globalist political culture, one that seeks to override nation states."

Immigrant bashing in America has been traditionally based more on economic fears, either of loss of jobs or of cultural change. Exacerbating those fears since 2001 and bringing many Americans closer to a European viewpoint has been the indelible mark that 9/11 has left on American consciousness. But in general, these fears are still somewhat economically based. And here we come to another story that easily shows how a nation of immigrants can easily be anti-immigrant.

In the early 1990s, a recessionary period in the United States with rising unemployment, my wife, Barbara G. Saidel, was volunteering to help Russian Jewish immigrants find jobs. She spoke at a branch of the Workmen's Circle, mainly senior citizens, explaining what she was doing and asking for help and references for any available jobs. The Workmen's Circle was an organization she grew up in that was made up of children, grandchildren, and great-grandchildren of Jewish immigrants from Russia and eastern Europe, a group one traditionally thinks of as celebrating immigration. The particular group she was speaking to, however, was amazingly anti-immigrant. The comments thrown at her were of the type, why should we help these people find jobs—essentially, why are they coming to New York—when our own children and grandchildren cannot find jobs?

Whether fear of immigration is historical, cultural, or economic, for the antiglobalist it is key. Immigration challenges people's concept of who and what their country is made up of; it challenges the age-old concept of tribe. It gets to the true heart of the populist antiglobalization argument, that countries in the process of economically aligning with each other for shared economic benefit are destroying their traditional character in the process. Of course, this argument is not based on rationality and ignores the fact that countries that do not evolve have historically lost their ability to compete in the world.

In addition to the direct economic stimulus associated with immigration that I wrote about earlier in this chapter, for the leading Western countries, controlled immigration is necessary just to stay economically even. As globalization has made countries richer, traditional domestic birth rates have substantially declined. Thus fewer young workers enter the workforce to replace older workers. Aging populations, combined with low birth rates, are probably the single common denominator among the leading industrial nations, the one exception being the United States. The question these countries face is how they can maintain their standard of living as the increase in retiring baby boomers starts to overtake the ability of the balance of the population to support boomer retirement while creating new economic growth.

In Japan more than 20 percent of the population is over sixty-five. The Japanese government estimates that if conditions stay on the same trajectory 40 percent of the population will be over sixty-five by 2060.

In Europe the situation is almost as bad. The European Commission stated, "The proportion of people of working age in the EU is shrinking while the relative number of those retired is expanding. The share of older persons in the total population will increase significantly in the coming decades which will lead to an increased burden on those of working age to provide for the social expenditure required by the aging population for a range of related services."

And this European situation here brings us to the importance of leadership in the globalization argument. Unlike Viktor Orbán in Hungary, Angela Merkel in Germany realized that without immigration Germany faces a severe fiscal problem in trying to maintain its traditional social safety net, as well as potentially facing a long-term decline in GDP.

Taking a huge political risk and showing amazing political courage, Merkel adopted an open-door policy, allowing more than one million refugees into Germany starting in 2015. Merkel's decision—made for both humanitarian reasons and for Germany's future economic health—caused a severe political pushback in the 2018 German elections for parliament. For the first time since World War II the German voters, in an apparent partial rebuke to Merkel's immigration stance, put a far-right party, the Alternative for Germany (AfD), in parliament. The AfD, campaigning against immigration, won 12.6 percent of the vote and more than ninety seats.

Interestingly, because of immigration the United States is in a better position than Europe in terms of declining birth rates. Of course, whether this advantage remains so, as the Trump administration continuously attacks immigration, is debatable. According to the *Fiscal Times*,

It's only because of immigration that the U.S. doesn't find itself in the same economic conundrum as Japan, China, South Korea, and Europe.

The U.S. is exceptionally young among OECD [Organization for Economic Cooperation and Development] nations; it's the country's immigrants that are keeping the population balanced and preventing it from becoming like Japan, Korea, and much of Europe.

Without immigration the U.S. would, in other words, have sub-replacement birth numbers like every other OECD nation. And it would, presumably, suffer a similar economic malaise caused in large measure by this demographic structural reconstruction of their populations.

And, according to United Nations, the U.S. is the only developed country expected to contribute to global population growth by 2050.

In a purely economic view of the world, controlled immigration makes perfectly logical sense, but as we have seen, rationality is a small part of human decision making, especially when it comes to immigration. To so many people in the United States and Europe, the words *immigrants* and *immigration* are strongly associated with a wider fear of cultural change, and supposed fear of economic competition.

In the United States, what I call "controlled immigration" should in principle not be difficult to get to through the legislative process. First, although Donald Trump has exploited the issue of open borders and made it one of fear and hate, the reality is that a country cannot guarantee the rule of law, promote the general welfare of its citizens, or even exist unless it can secure its borders. With the 1986 immigration reform, three million undocumented immigrants took advantage of the amnesty provision, but now that system appears to have totally broken down and in 2018 there were an estimated 10.5 million undocumented people living in the United States. Ironically, however, this number is down from its peak in 2007, when there were 12.2 million undocumented people living in the United States.

Second, it would be against all American values to kick these people out, and on the practical side it would cause economic harm and disruption. Thus law-abiding, hardworking undocumented immigrants need to be given a path to legal residency and citizenship, including paying back taxes, if for nothing else than a sense of fairness to the American citizens they have competed against.

Third, we should welcome immigration from all over the world, within the numbers Congress will agree to. The Statue of Liberty, not the "Halt" sign, should be synonymous with America. That being said, we should follow the German pattern, with all new immigrants having to take a compulsory integration course: six hundred hours of English lessons and one hundred hours of civics.

And last, we need to improve merit-based immigration and appreciate how important this is in the age of human capital. America's competitive advantage today is in knowledge-based industries, but like many issues, Congress has not caught up with the importance of global movements in human intellectual capital and with how they will affect these industries and the geopolitical standing of the United States. Members of Congress appear not to understand that knowledge-based human capital—that is, engineers, scientists, tech entrepreneurs, and the like—is the new hot commodity and represents an inflow of investment into the country.

So, although the United States in general allows unrestricted flows of actual capital into the country—known as foreign direct investment, such as Volkswagen building a plant in Tennessee—there are limits on the flow of modern-day capital—skilled engineers and tech workers—because of a far too low cap on H-1B visas, which allows U.S. employers to temporarily employ foreign workers in specialty occupations. The H-1B visa also eventually leads to permanent residency for many of these people. And then there is another easy and logical way to encourage human capital immigration, allowing foreign students who get an advanced degree in the United States to receive a green card along with their diploma.

In principle, reform of immigration should not be difficult to get through the legislative process in America. But in reality, it is almost impossible. Surely this problem does not call into question the survival of globalization, which is a given no matter what the U.S. Congress does. But what it does is raise the issue of whether the current form of representative government in the United States—or any representative democracy—is up to meeting the challenges that our current era of globalization presents. And here Angela Merkel's truly brave decision is an example. Merkel made a decision that would benefit Germany in the long term but in the short term would create some cultural conflict and force the German government to spend additional funds on settling and educating immigrants. Her decision almost cost her the chancellorship.

It is difficult to argue against the benefits of representative democracy, especially as issues become more complex. Unlike pure democracy, which, for example, makes decisions by referendum, a representative democracy offers time for consideration and for hearing all the facts, and, most important in a country as diverse as the United States, ensures the need for compromise.

Consider what happened in the United Kingdom with the very foolish idea to call a referendum on the very complex subject of withdrawing the UK from the European Union. Instead of allowing time for thinking through and exploring this very intricate question, the referendum turned out to be a war between tabloids goosed on by bots, Facebook, and other forms of social media. The truly difficult issues, those that didn't fit into a sound bite but that were the heart of the Brexit concept—such as what happens to the Irish border—were never part of the broad and simplistic discussion. And of course, other complicated questions never appeared on tabloid covers, like global fishing rights, an important but arcane issue which the United Kingdom now needs to renegotiate, this time without the overwhelming clout of the European Union. In total, there are over 750 treaties that the UK must now renegotiate without the powerful political and economic weight of the EU.

In the United States, except in a few statewide issues, traditional referendums per se are not the issue. The problem is the new marriage between social media, instant cable news, and sites like Twitter that pressure the government to take action before an issue is fully contemplated. Facebook and its imitators are the new referendums, directly challenging the concept of representative government. Adding to this problem is how easy it is for a leader to exploit social media by playing with half-truths to get around facts and move their own political agenda forward. In the process, a flawed message is disseminated to a partisan base and to the general public long before critical voices can challenge that message.

A prime example of this exploitation actually happened just as I was writing this book. Donald Trump tweeted out, "Russia and China are playing the Currency Devaluation game as the U.S. keeps raising interest rates. Not acceptable!" First his own Treasury Department directly contradicted this accusation in a report three days earlier and did not accuse either country of artificially lowering the value of its currency. Instead, the report showed that China's currency had moved up, which should benefit American exporters. Of course, the general public does not normally read publicly available Treasury Department reports. In fact, at the time of the tweet neither country was purposely devaluing its currency. Russia's currency was getting weaker because its economy was getting weaker and Russians were selling their rubles to get a more profitable and more stable return in investments outside Russia.

There was one truth in the president's tweet: the U.S. Federal Reserve Bank has been raising interest rates in the United States. But here is where the half-truth and the intellectual sleight of hand come in. Currencies that float against the dollar, meaning they can go up and down against the dollar in response to market pressures, normally fall in value when the United States raises its interest rates. This response is not because a foreign government—in this instance, Russia or China—devalued its currency but because with a rise in U.S. interest rates, traders will sell rubles or yuan to buy dollars, since the higher interest rate on the dollar allows them to get a better return.

There is one more sleight of hand in Trump's tweet. The message is that powerful countries, America's sometime adversaries Russia and China, are trading unfairly, shipping low-cost goods to the United States and manipulating their currency to do it. The problem here is that the United States has very little back-and-forth trade with Russia. In fact, the U.S trades more with Thailand and with Indonesia than it does with Russia. There is practically nothing Russia produces that the United States needs. It is apparent that President Trump put Russia in this tweet as a way of frightening people in reference to trade issues. Most Americans are probably not aware that Russia has a very small economy with few exports besides oil and gas, but of course they are aware, both from historic memory of the Cold War and because of Vladimir Putin's threatening actions, that Russia is dangerous.

This manipulation leads to the question, why is "governing by tweet" so effective in the United States during the second decade of the twenty-first century? First, as I discussed in many ways in the preceding chapters, we are living in a time when globalization, in the most stealthy manner, has radically changed the United States of America. Among other things it has caused a crisis of identity—a feeling of national insecurity that, in many ways, is more similar to Germany's prewar Weimar cynicism than to American optimism. And second, in the age of social media this insecurity is easy to manipulate and reinforce. Just think of a mathematical formula, with fear being the numerator and rapid change and globalization being the denominator, that equals political anxiety divided by the likelihood that people who have the most to lose by change will exploit the system to try to prevent change.

America's operating system, the Constitution, was written for the society and culture of 1787, not 2019. It was written not by the gods to last through eternity but by men dealing with a particular set of eighteenth-century problems. Just look how in the Constitution, each state gets two senators, a plan based on a 1787 concept of states' rights from a time when travel between the states was limited at best and people identified primarily with the state they lived in. But this concept today gives an overriding advantage not to the new areas of the American economy but to the most parochial areas of the economy. Does it make any sense today that Mississippi, with a GDP of $88.55 billion and only three million people, or Montana, which I referred to in chapter 4, have the same power in the U.S. Senate as California, with a GDP of $2.448 trillion and thirty-nine million people?

What has made the United States the creator of the knowledge age is its ability to adapt to change—ability derived from the United States' cultural respect for the freedoms to take risks, to innovate, and to be entrepreneurial. Innovation must bring about change, however, and change, as we have discussed, can be very threatening.

Without the American system of government that guarantees this freedom is open to all—and whose checks and balances ensure that any change will not be overly politically disruptive to society—

the United States would not be the great engine of innovation it is today. But for this guarantee of freedom to work, the political system cannot be held hostage by those who find a greater reward preserving the status quo indefinitely.

A system developed to rightfully protect the voice of the minority has now been manipulated so that the minority has not only rights but actual power over the majority. Three interlinked problems or situations have arisen over time that together seriously multiply the power of people who are not able or do not want to adapt to change. First, the primary system, which was originally developed in the latter part of the nineteenth century as a way of reforming how candidates are chosen, has evolved—especially in the Republican Party—as a blackmail tool against any elected official who advocates change. Since only a small percentage of the population votes in any primary, a small hardcore and passionate group of voters can determine the outcome, that is, who will be the candidate. It is irrelevant that this candidate does not represent the majority view; he or she must hold dear to the view of the hardcore primary voter if they themselves do not want to be primaried.

Second is the Supreme Court's ruling on *Citizens United vs.* FEC of January 21, 2010. In the decision, the court basically equated corporate campaign spending with freedom of speech, thus allowing interests most threatened by change to have a maximum voice. What is truly interesting about this decision is that the court did not limit power, which is something a conservative-based Supreme Court such as the one sitting at the time would normally do. Instead, apparently without considering the effect its decision would have on America's democratic tradition, it effectively granted the right of free speech, a massive power, to the highest bidder. In 1919 Supreme Court justice Oliver Wendell Holmes, defining the limits of free speech, famously said that you couldn't cry fire in a crowded theater. By equating free-for-all corporate campaign spending with free speech, the court in 2010 chose to ignore Holmes's dictum when it comes to America's democracy.

The last of the interlinked situations is gerrymandering, which essentially prevents changes by drawing the lines for an election district to benefit the incumbent. Gerrymandering on its own is fairly undemocratic, but when it is combined with the primary system, in essence it allows the primary, dominated by a small number of hardcore voters, to have the power of a general election.

These three actions, reinforced by "government by tweet," empower the minority beyond any concept the founders of the American Republic could have imagined. The interests of the status quo now have dominance over those advocating change. Whether the issue is taxes, energy, investments, or education, at a time when globalization is calling for immediate action, the U.S. government has become almost catatonic, trapped between the need for leadership and the empowerment of narrow factions.

The ultimate question is not whether globalization continues but whether the United States continues as its chief beneficiary. Or will rule by a fearful minority not only corrode America's democratic system of checks and balances but also cause it to lose its entrepreneurial advantage that helped lead it to globalization supremacy.

In 1977 Deng Xiaoping, the de facto leader of China, essentially changed the world when he stated, in response to the question of how he could dare experiment with capitalism in Maoist China, "I do not care if the cat is black or white. What matters is it catches mice." The statement was a true defense of economic pragmatism against ardent ideologues. It represented a Chinese version of the old American can-do spirit. It is as though Eli Whitney or Bill Gates or Warren Buffett had written the words for Deng.

But that American can-do spirit is now being checked. It is as if we have ceded economic pragmatism to the Chinese, who have run with it with astonishing speed while America is busy drowning in a quagmire of dogma. For a minority of Americans and especially for the current Republican leadership and the White House, it is more important to toe the so-called party line and to protect old or dying industries like steel or carbon-based sources of energy than it is to pragmatically approach the problems facing us. In America today, it does matter what color the cat is.

Paul Krugman describes this problem perfectly in a piece he wrote in his column in the *New York Times* on April 16, 2008, titled

"Earth, Wind and Liars." In the piece he goes into the huge strides in price competitiveness made by the alternative energy industry. He then states, in a powerful tell-it-like-it-is ending,

> But there is no longer any reason to believe that it would be hard to drastically "decarbonize" the economy. Indeed, there is no reason to believe that doing so would impose any significant economic cost. The realistic debate is about how hard it will be to get from 80 to 100 percent decarbonization.

For now, however, the problem isn't technology—it's politics.

The fossil fuel sector may represent a technological dead end, but it still has a lot of money and power. Lately it has been putting almost all of that money and power behind Republicans. For example, in the 2016 election cycle the coal mining industry gave 97 percent (!)of its contributions to G.O.P. candidates.

What the industry got in return for that money wasn't just a president who talks nonsense about bringing back coal jobs and an administration that rejects the science of climate change. It got an Environmental Protection Agency head who's trying to suppress evidence on the damage pollution causes, and a secretary of energy who tried, unsuccessfully so far, to force natural gas and renewables to subsidize coal and nuclear plants.

In the long run, these tactics probably won't stop the transition to renewable energy, and even the villains of this story probably realize that. Their goal is, instead, to slow things down, so they can extract as much profit as possible from their existing investments.

Unfortunately, this really is a case of "in the long run we are all dead." Every year that we delay the clean-energy transition will sicken or kill thousands while increasing the risk of climate catastrophe.

The point is that Trump and company aren't just trying to move us backward on social issues; they're also trying to block technological progress. And the price of their obstructionism will be high.

Of course, interest groups protecting their power by gaming the system are not a new phenomenon in American history. The late 1800s are full of examples of the Rockefellers, Fiskes, and Morgans manipulating the legislative and court system to protect their wealth and power. But in the late 1800s a successful political coalition also arose against monopolization and oligarchies: the reform movement.

Theodore Roosevelt and then Woodrow Wilson, assisted by numerous muckrakers, used the presidency as a bully pulpit and created the reforms needed not only to rebalance the system but also to enable the United States to move forward into the twentieth century.

Decision making in a democracy is partly about appeasing different constituencies, including people who benefit from the existing system and people who are left behind and are frightened by the future. To create a majority coalition for reform, some of these people need to be convinced that the future will be better than the past.

But to do that, clear leadership needs to exist to support reform. Which leads to probably the key question for the United States in the first quarter of the twenty-first century. Can an environment for reform succeed against the pressure of the now institutionalized fear-based power of the minority—the primary system, Citizens United, gerrymandering—all dramatically amplified by twenty-four-hour talking heads, cable T V, and government by tweet.

It is rare in history for the hegemon, in this case the United States and the postwar multilateral rules-based trade system, purposely to withdraw from the international system it created and turn its back on it. Of course, the United States has withdrawn into isolationism before, in particular after World War I, but at that time America was far from being recognized as a global hegemon, the global cop.

Today, isolationism, closing oneself off from the world, motivated by both fear and the power of vested interests, can only have one result, the decline of America.

With a wonderful quote from Lee Kuan Yew, the first prime minister of Singapore and the man who was an informal adviser to Deng Xiaoping on capitalism, Joseph Nye, the former dean of the Kennedy School of Government at Harvard University, in an April 9,

2018, article in Project Syndicate, simply and succinctly states the vital importance of openness to America: "I once asked him [Lee Kuan Yew] about whether China would surpass the US. He said 'no,' because while China had the talents of 1.4 billion people to draw upon, the openness of the US allowed it to tap and combine the talents of 7.5 billion people with greater creativity than China could. If that openness survives, American leadership in Asia, and elsewhere, will most likely survive as well."

Ironically, up until now the main example of a hegemon withdrawing from the world is China and that was almost five hundred years ago in the early 1500s. Zheng He, the great Chinese admiral with crews consisting of almost twenty-eight thousand men and a fleet of sixty-two treasure ships supported by 190 smaller ships, opened trade throughout the Indian Ocean, going as far as the Straits of Hormuz and Aden in Yemen. After Zheng He's death, his immediate successors were ordered to stop expanding trade routes and to stop dealing with the outside world. To ensure that this order would be carried out, the Chinese government in 1525 ordered the destruction of all ocean-going ships.

So what happens when you close yourself off from the world? After the destruction of the fleet, China slowly declined until the mid-nineteenth century, when it turned into the plaything of the European powers. And here is where another historic irony takes place; the Europeans had begun exploring the world at approximately the same time that China withdrew from the world. Europe in the 1400s was significantly poorer than China, but by the 1900s, Europe, with its ruling culture of exploration and globalization, was able to dominate China.

Without the clout of America's leadership, the concept of globalization weakens dramatically, not as an evolutionary force but as pragmatic geopolitical arrangements for nations to remain peaceful and prosper. History shows that when the hegemon chooses to isolate itself from the world, geopolitical relations fall back into the old idea of balance of power and realpolitik, a theory based on the concept that countries form pacts, alliances, or blocs of military and economic power so that no single major country is strong enough to be an aggressor against an opposing bloc.

There are some who will argue that balance of power is a natural way to ensure peace. But these same people generally forget how "successful" the balance-of-power concept was in preventing both world wars. The theory worked somewhat effectively during the Cold War, but that was when there were only two rival superpowers, each possessing the ability to annihilate the other. Globalization offers a simpler way to maintain long-term peace among great powers: trade creates economic interdependence, binding the supplier to the customer, and vice versa. Blocs in theory are not necessary because you have interconnected trade relations. You have what Parag Khanna, a CNN global contributor and a senior research fellow in the Center on Asia and Globalization at the Lee Kuan Yew School of Public Policy, calls the power of connectivity.

This is not to say that globalization, as a way of maintaining peace among the great powers and blocs, is a perfectly frictionless system. Obviously it is not. Just look at the European Union, which is essentially ground zero of the globalist concept that historical enemies united by trade can prosper together instead of being destructive belligerents. Of course the European Union has had its up and downs, but these are historically minor. Its major premise, starting with a declaration in 1949 by its historical founder, French prime minister Schuman, that economic ties can bind nations together, has held up against all historic precedents remarkably well. For sure globalization has caused severe economic and cultural disruption that, if not dealt with beneficially by a country's domestic political system, causes globalization itself to be the enemy. That is why France's current leader, President Emmanuel Macron, stated that he is for protection, not protectionism.

Certainly there are countries, aspiring powers, and leaders that will see the domestic destabilization that unprotected globalization can cause as an opportunity to amass power. Look at Vladimir Putin, who could easily be labeled the czar of chaos, the king of entropy. Russia as it exists today is the singular loser in the game of globalization, having essentially gone economically backward. In the commercial world of globalization, Russia's main product, oil, is rapidly becoming yesterday's product, and since oil was always a take-it-or-leave-it product, the Russian economy never needed to develop the entrepreneurial skills to sell other products to the world.

For Putin, power is in disrupting the globalized world. Russia's strength is in the old geography-based balance-of-power game. For in that game, Russia, with a declining population and a small economy, can be a player. Russia's attributes fit perfectly for this, since it has the world's largest land mass, the second-largest nuclear arsenal in the world, borders on all the hot spots in the world as well as Europe and China, and has a veto in the United Nations Security Council.

Unlike Trump, who is willing to disregard America's comparative advantage in globalization for personal political gain, Putin appears to have realized that the old realpolitik/ balance-of-power foreign concept of foreign policy is the only game where Russia, a corrupt and economically backward nation can demonstrate power on the world stage. Of course Trump and Putin are not the only leaders who see their countries or political positions becoming more secure by attacking globalization. The leaders of Poland and Hungary, and of course Turkey, for one reason or another see a benefit in disrupting the globalized system.

For Trump, the appeal of both isolationism and the old balance-of-power game is that they are convenient domestic political tools to rally political support. A bad-guy/good-guy view of the world is much easier to sell and explain to your base than trade agreements or sharing of power. A trade agreement could hurt a small minority or a vested interest group, but the bad-guy/good-guy view in its simplicity hurts no one, at least on the surface.

This approach of course totally ignores how America and the world have changed economically. Look at how the midwestern agricultural states and the automobile industry have pushed back against the Trump Administration's aggressive positions on China trade and the renegotiation of the NAFTA treaty. The U.S.-Chinese situation is a perfect example of how globalized economic interdependence dissuades the two parties from conflict. In a preglobalized world, the Trumpian rhetoric on China would have moved both countries close to war, in a situation similar to that of pre-

World War I Germany and England. Today both the United States and China appear to have too much economically to lose.

And most important, a balance-of-power strategy for securing peace and prosperity does not play to America's strengths against the massive population and new economic power of China. But a globalized strategy does. Just think about the idea of tangible versus intangible assets that I wrote about in chapter 4, the old fixed, localized steel mill versus the globalized market of Google. America's belief in meritocracy, when shaken together with the melting pot of immigration and a strong jolt of intellectual freedom, is a unique but unquantifiable advantage in the globalized world. In a time when ideas are power and money, it is this blend of diverse thought and multiculturalism that acts as America's catalyst for maintaining its dominant position in a globalized world. Human capital is the new oil, and no other major country has this key economic and intellectual advantage.

And remarkably this is an advantage China, the former poster child of globalization, has now ceded to the United States. With President Xi's ever-increasing insistence on political correctness, on adhering to the party line and moving to the tech version of big-brother control of thought within China, it is easy to speculate how China could be moving into a historic period similar to when Zheng He's great fleet was destroyed. Party control in China now seems more important than Deng's black-and-white cats. And with that control, intellectual competitiveness, and sharing of ideas, no matter where they originate, the keystones of a human-capital-based world will become more difficult in China.

So the question becomes, what happens if through the pressure of antiglobalist politics and short-term political gain, America knowingly gives up the leadership of globalization to an ever-increasing autocratic China? Does globalization go from a game that benefited most people around the world to a game, absent American leadership, of one-road-to-China?

In a world satiated with technology yet short of natural resources, where globalization has caffeinated the massive societies of China and India and parochialism is in open rebellion, will the counterrevolution lead to a period similar to pre–World War I economic nationalism, combined with some new form of authoritarianism? Or can globalization, which has truly been beneficial not only to the majority of Americans but also to the majority of the world, be harnessed in order to preserve democracy as we know it?

At the moment, we are in a race between democracy and authoritarianism, between globalization and nationalism. Globalization, as I said, will win as it has always done, but how democracy finishes in this race, and how America can continue to be the dynamic entrepreneurial economy it is, are other questions entirely.

A Separate Peace, John Knowles's wonderful coming-of-age novel about two friends, ends with these staccato-like lines: "All of them, constructed at infinite cost to themselves, these Maginot Lines against this enemy they thought they saw across the frontier, this enemy who never attacked that way—if he ever attacked at all." I don't know if any of the antiglobalist leaders in America have ever read *A Separate Peace*, but I do know this: they are building Maginot Lines of defense around the United States of America—as if such a defense could protect America from tomorrow and return it to what they believe it was.